FROM OLD NOTEBOOKS

FROM OLD NOTEBOOKS

EVAN LAVENDER-SMITH

BlazeVOX [books]
Buffalo, New York

Published by BlazeVOX [books]

Printed in the United States of America

Book design by Thus Roithamer

ISBN: 9781935402855
Library of Congress Control Number: 2009941029

BlazeVOX [books]
303 Bedford Ave
Buffalo, NY 14216

Editor@blazevox.org

publisher of weird little books

BlazeVOX [books]

blazevox.org

2   4   6   8   0   9   7   5   3   1

Even now, whenever I accidentally touch this book, almost every sentence turns for me into a net that again brings up from the depths something incomparable: its entire skin trembles with tender thrills of memory. The art that distinguishes it is not inconsiderable when it comes to fixing to some extent things that easily flit by, noiselessly—moments I call divine lizards—but not with the cruelty of that young Greek god who simply speared the poor little lizard, though, to be sure, with something pointed—a pen.

Nietzsche

Short story about a church on the ocean floor. Congregation in scuba gear.

Memoir in which narrator struggles to describe her childhood—offering two or more contrary accounts of the same event—having been raised by divorced parents with unresolved anger toward each other such that discrepancies between parents' accounts of each other's involvement in her childhood have damaged narrator's memory beyond repair.

Academic essay entitled "*Cute Title: Serious Subtitle*: On the Preponderance of Precious Subtitling in Academic Essays."

Novel in chapters, each chapter spanning one year, 1977–2006. In lieu of chapter number, photograph of Tom Cruise's face from that year.

Story about a garbage man who cannot fathom how anyone might be content living a life not wholly dedicated to being a garbage man.

Something entitled "Born Dead." Or "Born Died."

Novel that suffers from the Y2K bug. iPods all the craze in 1906, etc.

Short story about someone living inside of a piano.

Short story about a male professor whose academic specialty is representations of female prostitutes in novels and films. One day after class he sneaks away to a hotel room on the outskirts of town in order to experience, firsthand, the forbidden delights of real live prostitute sex, to finally *defeat the hooker simulacrum*. But the prostitute, upon learning that the skinny balding man struggling to unbutton her blouse is a literature professor, becomes eager to chat about novels and films, especially those containing representations of female prostitutes. She suggests that these films and books have strongly influenced the way she *performs* being a prostitute; the professor passionately insists she is mistaken; she demurs; argument ensues; prostitute finally stands up for herself with all the clichéd self-regard of prostitutes in novels and films, storms out of the hotel room.

Novel in which the verb *to be* and all inflections thereof appear italicized in every instance.

Scene from a film in which Steven Spielberg carries his severed arm across a war-torn battlefield.

Essay arguing that Aaron Copland is the best American composer.
    Essay arguing that Aaron Copland is the worst American composer.

Screenplay in which screenwriter includes a cast list with Hollywood stars cast in improbable roles:

Arnold Schwarzenegger   TRANSVESTITE PROSTITUTE
Bruce Willis   DEAD GUY IN MORGUE
Angelina Jolie   LEPER
Jim Carrey   DRIVE-BY SHOOTER

Julia Roberts   CRACK WHORE #1
Tom Cruise   CRACK WHORE #2

Novel about a haunted cryonics storage facility.

Memoir beginning with detailed narrative description of subject's rich and fertile childhood slowly disintegrates into list of difficult books he read as an adult.

Reality television show in which ten writers living in the same house compete for a two-book deal.

Novella in which protagonist, sitting in a chair at the airport waiting to pick up old friend who never arrives, looks down at feet to find laptop case. Decides to leave airport with, if not old friend, laptop. At home, discovers directory on hard drive with 30 folders inside, each named a year (1977–2006); within each of those, twelve more folders; within each of those, 28–31 folders; within each of those, 24 folders; within each of those, 60 folders; within each of those, anywhere from 1–60 .txt files. Opens one of the .txt files to find what seems a bunch of gibberish—*like contemporary poetry*, he thinks to himself—opens another and another, all the same, but occasionally certain words seem familiar: the first name of his girlfriend appears, or the word *death* appears alongside the names of streets he regularly drives on or foods he regularly eats. Protagonist slowly comes to realize laptop contains textual transliterations of his own thoughts from those moments in time. Novella alternates between narrative account of finding laptop, slowly discovering therein a file structure corresponding to his life, etc.; and *Principia*-type laws he derives about the file structure. E.g:

> *Law 3* Any break in the contiguity of the file structure's numeration represents a period during which I was unconscious, that is, not producing recallable thought-data.

> *Law 4* The current rate of file growth is inversely proportional to my current rate of conscious thought.

At story's end protagonist sits reading his thoughts from story's beginning, story's middle, story's end.

Academic essay, after Moretti, quantifying the extent to which Jackson Pollock's paintings influenced late-20th-century hairstyles.

Story about a mother who develops an allergic reaction to her kids.

"The boy lost the spelling bee on the word *metrorrhagia* and cried all the way home."

Short story in which the most crucial plot details are divulged in footnotes, the most trivial details in narration.

Character whose job is to talk people down from manic fear-of-death episodes.

Pamphlet quantifying the difficulties of quitting smoking v. quitting drinking.

Baby in story chokes on errant outlet cover, dies.

Short story in which protagonist becomes addicted to drugs because he has a drug-bully friend who appears to suffer tremendous affront upon protagonist's suggestion, "Maybe we should call it a night," such that it seems to protagonist their relationship will suffer irreparably if he doesn't stay out all night with drug bully, doing all sorts of drugs.

Story about a child who excitedly goes to see a 3-D movie, but his *strabismus* prevents him from looking through bo-

lenses simultaneously, so he sees the movie in either 2-D blue or 2-D red. A huge theater, everyone around him *ooohing* and *aaahing*, flinching, throwing their heads back in unison. Child sitting motionless. Getting up, excusing himself from aisle. Hurriedly exiting auditorium, finding a bathroom, locking himself in a stall, weeping.

Short story about a world in which fear of death is physically infectious.

Satiric essay/story in the form of a reality-show contract.

Title of Carmen's hypothetical self-help book for new mothers: *How to Take a Shit While Holding Your Baby*.

Something called "Shivering in the Sun."

How as a child I once felt that everyone but me was an automaton. —As I sometimes feel still, except for that *but me*.

Just because/ I dream about/ Tom Cruise/ doesn't mean/ he dreams about/ me. Just because I/ dream about Tom/ Cruise doesn't mean/ he dreams/ about me. Just/ because I/ dream about Tom/ Cruise doesn't/ mean he/ dreams about me.

Something entitled "The Pleasures of Consciousness."

Character whose dog's name is Virgule.

Dying character's last words: "I wish I would have eaten more fruit! God how I wish I would have eaten more fruit!"

Scene in which a father tells his son that his—the father's— penis is slightly smaller than average, and that the son should expect for his penis to be the same.

When I look down to find my T-shirt hiked up, my boxer shorts ballooning out over my belt.

In high school, when I *bagged my pants* and wore extra-large shirts, a friend one day alerted me to this same condition, so pronounced on this day that when I sat down on a concrete bench outside the cafeteria, my shirt bunched up around my waist to reveal a section of pure bare thigh below my boxer shorts, above my pants.

Something called "The Misanthropic Principle."

Essay describing the structure of *Infinite Jest* as Hofstadterian *strange loop*, the novel's structure being that of a circle with a missing section—between the last and first pages—which must be *filled in* by the reader who has been, by the end of the novel, prepared, practiced, coached to do so, just as life allegedly teaches one how to die.

Short story about a career Bookmobile driver.

Character who ejaculates on dollar bills before setting them back into circulation.

By waving my hands before my face I effect physical processes of unfathomable complexity.
   —As I do when thinking of nothing at all.

When reading something I greatly admire, pretending I wrote it. Reading something I greatly admire, pretending I wrote it, and pretending I'm someone other than myself who's greatly admiring it while reading it. Pretending I'm Tom Waits's best friend. Reading something I've written and pretending an author I greatly admire has written it.

Monologue spoken by an aging pianist-composer, based on Prokofiev, beginning with the following sentence: *My fingers have grown very tired.*

Something entitled "From Old Notebooks," simply a transcription of entries from these notebooks.

Story involving a couple whose divorce proceedings center upon the allocation of the books contained in the family library.

Living off-campus on the outskirts of a city where I knew no one, in a studio apartment the size of a large walk-in closet, I would occupy myself in the evenings with an obsessive study of the shadows of my hands against the wall as I faux-conducted piano concertos; and later, after having taken three Ambien, intimate conversations with bits of magma crawling across the carpet that had detached from the glowing wires on my electric space heater. That same year, in a fit of manic loneliness, I invited a raccoon into my apartment with a trail of cracker crumbs.

Do not let Jackson and Sofia live off-campus as undergraduates.

Cached auto-complete entry options that appear when I type the letter *e* into the search field in the toolbar of my internet browser:

> *evan lavender-smith*
> *"evan lavender-smith"*
> *"evan lavender smith"*
> *evan +"lavender-smith"*
> *evan +"lavender smith"*
> *evan +lavender +smith*

The letter *f*:

> *fear of death*

Contemporary authors who construct a thick barrier between themselves and their readers such that *authorial vulnerability* is revealed negatively, i.e., via the construction of the barrier.

If Team USA had a mascot, it would be God.

Character who refers to Wellbutrin as his muse.

"I hope to one day storm out on Terry Gross during an interview because I am that kind of eccentric famous author."

Story about a character who goes around knocking on the front doors of strange houses, claiming to have once lived there, receiving gracious tours.

Artists who take comfort in the potential posthumous legacy of their art must forget they have no chance of cheating *death* but only *oblivion*, and that only for a moment.

James Joyce might seem to me less dead than most dead but to him he is just as dead as all the rest.

How it took Carmen and me more than two years to call Jackson by his real name, how many ridiculous nicknames we shuffled through—*Buttbutt, Buttface, Angelbuttface, Bean, Beanbutt, Beaner, Beanie, Beaniebutt, Beaniebuttface*—before recently landing on his real name.

How, after two months, we've called Sofia only *Baby Sista* or *Beanetta*.

"Mr. Lavender-Smith, welcome back. It's been nearly 850 billion years since you were last alive. How are we feeling this morning?"

Removing a copy of Saramago's *The Gospel According to Jesus Christ* from the shelf at Barnes & Noble to find all pages inside blank—either a printer's error or joke—purchasing the book anyway, taking it off my shelf from time to time to thumb through it.

Short story about a psychotherapist who sues his client, a novelist, for stealing and plagiarizing his ideas.

My response to Carmen's apprehension when I told her I planned to use her real name in "From Old Notebooks": "What, are you scared to be immortalized or something?"

The suggestion that *Ulysses* might someday be considered the final part of a trilogy beginning with the Old and New Testaments.

"Old people with tennis balls on the feet of their walkers, the pretentious bastards."

When taking the garbage out to the street on Wednesday nights I shield the sky and stars from my eyes with my hand so to not spark needless ontological distress and ruin my evening.

My grandfather is born, my great-grandfather dies, my father is born, my grandfather dies, I am born, my father dies, my son is born, I die, my grandson is born, my son dies, my great-grandson is born, my grandson dies.

Story about a character whose mother attempts suicide the day following a major argument between them. The son stands firm and continues to ignore her.

The next issue of *McSweeney's* printed on the exterior of its cardboard shipping box. The next issue of *McSweeney's* printless, recited to subscriber by mailman.

The next issue of *McSweeney's* printed on a roll of toilet paper.

My second worst fear would have to be *telephonophobia*, fear of telephones, specifically, fear of talking on telephones. It's rather difficult, however, to distinguish between my actual fear of talking on telephones and my affectation of my fear of talking on telephones. As if my telephonophobia were at once entirely sincere and totally fake.

Stressed-out mother in story prescribed Xanax for anxiety, begins crushing up pills, sprinkling in kids' cereal. As kids' tolerance increases, mother ups the dosage. Etc., etc.

I feel comfortable putting off *getting spiritual* for another 15 years just as I feel comfortable putting off *getting in shape* for another 15 years.

"It makes no difference to me where or how I live so long as I have my family by my side, my wife and children." Meditative pause. "And of course my books." Another. "And my porn."

"Dada doing?"
    "Just trying to kill this fly."
    "Dada killing?"

My after-meal cigarette, my *post-prandial*.

Someone said that the color white does not exist in nature, but that someone did not see my son or daughter's skin in the first moments after birth.

A moment of exquisite romance, Gloucester asking his son to lead him toward a cliff for the purpose of committing suicide.

From Old Notebooks. If only to make a record of a very important period in my life before I forget the details, the sounds and the smells.

After dating my high school girlfriend for over a year without engaging in physical activity beyond *macking*, one day I wore shorts—rarely did I wear shorts back then—and, as we lay in the backseat of my car *sucking face*, she reached into one of my shorts' legs to commence my life's first-ever *hand-job*.

When it was over, I said, sincerely, "I should wear shorts more often."

Memoir which is a scratch-and-sniff affair.

It is alarming to pull something out of the fridge to find that its expiration date elapsed in the previous century.

In our day-to-day use of the English language we possess a perfect record of the language's evolution; when we hear ourselves speak we listen to the voices of all those many millions who have come before us, who have, in their own use of the language, constructed ours, as we continue to construct it.

Whether or not we're able to decipher this record is another matter altogether.

Short short story about a trio of preteens hiding in bushes next to the green of a blind Par 3, waiting for golf balls to land, scrambling to gather balls and place them all in the hole before golfers arrive, diving back into bushes, waiting expectantly.

"I need to sit down and catch my breath, i.e., have a cigarette."

I took my brother to a strip club on his sixteenth birthday and he fainted while receiving a lap dance.

That same night a man with Down's syndrome waited in line to give a dancer a dollar. Holding a bare breast in each hand, she bent down to grasp the dollar bill in her cleavage; the retarded man spit the dollar from his mouth and bit her on the nipple. She yelped and slapped him, stood on stage crying with a trickle of blood on her breast.

The countless hours I have spent scrutinizing grout lines in public bathrooms.

Novelization of the film *Weekend at Bernie's*.

The wonderment when someone first revealed three nymphs crowded around a man's erect penis within the drawing of the camel on a pack of Camel cigarettes.

"No diaper, Dada. It's just a fart."

A rhyming abridgement of *Ulysses*. For children.

Two days without a cigarette. Two days without drinking.
Three days without a cigarette. Three days without drinking.
Two days without a cigarette. Two days without drinking.

From Old Notebooks: A Memoir.
From Old Notebooks: A Novel.
From Old Notebooks: A Memoivel.

Title of my dream autobiography: *Hookers & Blow*.

How I feel proximity to Bloom such that when I read "Then he read the letter again: twice," I perceive a violence upon the contiguity of his consciousness to mine, and my eyes must return to the beginning of the letter: twice.

Pouring a tumbler of Jameson too late in the day—7 PM, already time for beer—unable to find the funnel, hiding the glass on my desk behind a stack of books, for tomorrow. Or for after beer.

Is there some critical mass of the number of human consciousnesses that must exist before a single human consciousness will, through physical chance alone, be repeated?

Of course not.

When jazz musicians have symphony orchestras at their disposal.

No matter how I live my life, they will either say, *He lived a very good life*, or, *He lived a very sad life*.

Something called "The Thinking Man's Pimp."

Story about two dogs in a backyard, J-Lo and Ben, the former always sneaking off and jumping the fence to get some action from neighborhood dogs.

Since having children my handwriting has taken a dramatic turn for the worse.

"With my first book I hope to get all the cult of personality stuff out of the way."

Wittgenstein's proposition that the immortality of the soul would be no less enigmatic, no less inexplicable than mortal existence—which remains the single most disturbing reading experience of my life, having had hitherto placed all my eggs in the basket of the promise of immortality—may be an example of a startling thought that will seem perfectly obvious to the children of the future, as the cogito seemed to us when we were kids.

How after we buried Sara in the backyard all the other dogs of the neighborhood came and sat together on a hill overlooking her grave.

"Dada, where moon?"
    "I think it's a new moon tonight."
    "Huh?"
    "It's a new moon, hon. I'm sorry."
    "Huh?"

"I'm sorry, sweetie, but I don't think there'll be a moon tonight."

"Oh, Dada! My so sad!"

Marcus Roberts's left hand in the E-flat-minor section of "The Entertainer" may suggest something fundamental about the condition of being a blind musician.

Seven-year-old Drew from next door who drowned when his hand got caught in the drainpipe on the floor of his swimming pool while we were away on family vacation. Upon learning of his death, Mom saying, "If only we hadn't been on vacation, maybe we would've heard him screaming and been able to do something to save him." Dad, "But we wouldn't have been able to hear him. He was underwater, at the bottom of the pool."

Surely I'm misremembering.

Story entitled "M" about two men attempting to scale the heights of the letter *M*.

Do philosophers who write in the aphoristic mode contradict themselves *of necessity*?

The entries in *From Old Notebooks* are the shadows cast by my life, which is the story just beyond the reach of the book.

The entries are the evidence of story?

The mistaken notion I've carried with me my whole life—and continue to carry with me despite my certainty that it is entirely mistaken—that things with me will generally turn out OK, that things concerning me and my life and things concerning those people I care about will in the end work themselves out for the best. Although this entirely mistaken notion continues to be reinforced day in and day out, I do not doubt that it is entirely mistaken, that it is in fact *the very opposite* of what will happen—everything will work itself out for the absolute *worst*, everyone I care about will *die*—and yet somehow I go about my life actually believing in this nonsense.

The women I've been with in my life have displayed an aptitude for armchair adjectivizing: *strappy, schticky, sucky, skanky, crampy, trampy, headachey, boutiquey, colicky, pee-em-essy, salady, garlicky, lemongrassy, swimsuity . . .*

The apparent influence of *Notes from Underground* on so many of my favorite novels.

—"The Ranting Cellar Dweller; or, From Dostoyevsky to Bernhard."

Once again feeling emasculated by the Network Connection Wizard.

In a Mexican brothel with members of my MFA class, a bouncer led us and two middle-aged prostitutes out the back door, through an alley, down a staircase, into a different building, through a hallway and into a poorly lit bedroom where we watched the prostitutes perform a sex show *from around the world*, showing us how they do it in *France*, in *Morocco*, in *Greece*. . . . The sheets on the bed were Spongebob Squarepants, a curious detail then, but now . . . *Were we in a child's bedroom?*

Patches/gum for alcohol addiction.

A play which presents the goings-on of the backstage of a play, the stage of which is, ostensibly, the backstage of our play. Characters are hurled from our backstage (their stage) onto our stage (their backstage). Our stage (their backstage) is a barren, apocalyptic wasteland of no hope. Every moment they are on our stage (their backstage), characters yearn to return to their stage (our backstage).

How incommodious to belong to such a self-conscious species.

How I used to imagine women peeing in a deluge rather than a stream.

At the age of six I fell asleep holding a teddy bear . . . at sixteen holding a book . . . at twenty-six holding a woman nursing a baby . . . at twenty-eight holding a toddler holding a teddy bear, a book, and a woman nursing a baby.

Mock interview with "Larry Peters, Dallas Maverick and American Poet," beginning with the following question: "You were awarded last year's NBA Rookie of the Year Award as well as the Yale Younger Poets Prize for your book *Reasoning the Fruit*. How do you manage to get poetry written with such a rigorous road schedule hanging over your head?"

A good way to characterize my insomnia might be to say it's like trying to sleep five minutes after snorting a line of cocaine.

The major strength and fault of *Ulysses* being its manner of representation of direct thought, a technique which stands as perhaps the grandest conceit in the history of literature.
   —Because people don't actually think that way!
   —Except for maybe Joyce?

Short story in which reclusive protagonist's stash of pornography keeps mysteriously vanishing.

Does my anxiety follow from conceptual death, Death, or my own personal death?

But what is the difference, really?

Many philosophers alert us to the limitations of science in one of two ways, haughtily or offhandedly, just as many scientists alert us to the limitations of philosophy in one of two ways, haughtily or offhandedly.

The scientist and philosopher are like identical twins in a world without mirrors.

PBS program entitled "Pimp My Vita."

Marquee outside Las Cruces Biologicals: "Need money for gas? Donate plasma!"

Blood for oil.

Upon my suggestion that I don't have to worry about my drinking and smoking because of the advances medical science will undergo in the upcoming decades, Carmen: "You know you have a pretty science-fictiony attitude about your health."

How Justin's dad told Justin and me he'd finally decided not to have his head sawed off and frozen in order to return to life hundreds or thousands of years later, when technology would permit his *reanimation*, because it had suddenly occurred to him he wouldn't be able to stand being alive if his children were dead.

The suggestion being that Justin and his sisters need to get with the program and make the decision to have their heads sawed off and frozen.

Short story about married couple with very staid sex life. Wife secretly desperate for sexual adventure, pays strong black men to await husband's return from work, tackle him and bind his hands, blindfold him, lead him to basement where they and wife perpetrate outlandish sexual offenses against him. Men depart and wife reveals herself.

Wife returns to life of sexual repression, satisfied—for the nonce.

My anxiety about subject matter coming across as *cute*, and the shame I feel about why I choose to write what I do, when perceiving it as such. Worse, the shame of feeling I'm being *cute in my thinking*.

Derrida for Dummies.
    Foucault for Retards.

When Justin's dad told Justin and me that had we been born just a couple of decades later we'd have probably belonged to *the immortal generation*, how terribly upset we became.

Pornographic film entitled *The Oxford Companion to Pussy.*

The Illusion of Improvisation in American Literature from Kerouac to Lavender-Smith.

"More rubba back, Dada. My ready night-night. More rubba back please."

    "I'll rub your back for two more minutes and then it's time for night-night, okay?"

    "Okay, Dada. More rubba back, Dada. One hour rubba back."

Carmen calling me at work, sobbing. "Jackson slapped me and I slapped him back." Having imagined this as the one occasion upon which I'm allowed to *slap my wife's face*—my life's great romantic moment of domestic violence—I rush home to embrace her first and Jackson second.

What if there were a chef with genius comparable to Joyce's? What would his food taste like? Eating it, I might feel that until that moment I had never eaten real food.

Story about a father who is overly generous with sons. Sons not greedy but also not unwilling to accept father's generosities, which border on the grotesque. As father keeps giving, sons grow distant. Noticing, father increases pace of giving, until there's nothing left to give, until he's given away everything. Sons no longer come by, no longer call. Father alone, penniless. —Perfectly content?

Were I to write a philosophical treatise on a single subject it would best be on *cowardice*.

"And what do you do?"
   "I'm a poet."
   "Ah, a poet—I'd love to read some of your poetry."
   "Sorry, I only write prose."

Justin had an ulcer at the age of 8, "because of the Cold War."

Sequel to Barthelme's "The School." First line: *The children cheered wildly*. Story describes children's contented long-term relationship with gerbil.

The dirt under Sofia's fingernails is actually three months worth of dead skin dug from Carmen's chi-chis.

"H–E–double-hockey-sticks."

The limited content of Sequoia's dreams, my having never exposed her to very much more of the world than the tiny corner of it which is our dogshit-laden backyard.

Short story about a ban on baggy pants at a high school from the point of view of the somber baggy-pants inspector.

Novel entitled *The Wigger Par Excellence*.

So much of philosophy is one philosopher talking shit about another.

I now suspect that the new intensity of my fear of death was activated by Wellbutrin, originally prescribed to alleviate what I considered at the time to be the new intensity of my fear of death, but which, as it turns out, hardly qualified as intense.

Listening to someone perform an *innovative* close reading on a text can be boring in the same way as listening to someone recount her dreams.

When I first saw a pornographic photograph of a black woman, spread-eagled, same color inside as a white woman.

One of Sofia's favorite pastimes is pulling out Carmen's nose ring, watching Carmen push it back in, pulling it out again, watching Carmen push it in, pulling it out, watching. . . . It's a good metaphor for parenting.

How I keep thinking *ticker tape* as a metaphor for the relationship of the entries in F.O.N. to my life.
 A relationship of staggered correspondence.
 An isomorphic relationship.

Character who refers to *Ulysses* as his only friend.

One of the great rewards of having children: asking for a magazine while on the toilet.

Short film: Wal-Mart, late at night, dairy aisle: carton of eggs shakes, stops, shakes: lid flips open: egg breaks, baby chick emerges, falls from carton to aisle: bloody and squirming.

Character who suffers realization that father, a conscientious objector, must have answered in the negative to a question similar to the following: If an armed intruder entered your home, placed a gun to your son's temple and said, *Now I am going to shoot your son in the head*, and you had a chance to shoot and kill the intruder before he shot your son, would you?

How rare is the novel that really thinks about thinking, the novel, like *Ulysses*, determined to portray human thought in all its glory, all its mundanity.

How I'd enter someone's house to find a bong on the coffee table and immediately become disillusioned, knowing I'd either have to smoke from it and sacrifice all well-being, or say sheepishly, awkwardly, "None for me, thanks." How I'd enter someone's house to find a line of white powder on the coffee table and immediately begin visualizing the contents of my wallet, praying I'd brought a crisp dollar bill with me.

Story in which narrator, a porn connoisseur, describes scene-by-scene reactions, physical and critical, to a pornographic film he's recently seen.

How I never knew if it was called a *carve* or a *carb* so would always try to pronounce it somewhere in between.

Novel/film that takes place entirely inside automobiles.

The form of F.O.N. accommodating anything and everything I can think to write.

There is a day in the year, already passed 28 times without my knowing it, which is my *deathday*.

"Dada, hold you."

Novels with lots of *italicization*.

How I've once again substituted addictions, in this case given up going to casinos only to immerse myself in submitting short stories to literary journals.

Chances are the last thing I ever think about will be death.

"How similar is the Evan Lavender-Smith depicted in *From Old Notebooks* to the Evan Lavender-Smith from your day-to-day life?"

"Not at all. The real Evan Lavender-Smith has never been able to make it past the second episode of *Ulysses*, the real Evan Lavender-Smith has no children . . ."

Carmen, "Robert Hass might be one of two or three poets alive today who will still be read in a hundred years," to which I replied, "Too bad I didn't know that when I took his class; I might have gone to visit him in his office hours."

If someone put a gun to my head and said, "Suck your own dick or I'll put a bullet in your head," *then* would I be able to?

Character in story keeps a ledger in which he records the number of times per day the wind is knocked out of him following from his apprehension of the fact of death.

Something called "The Cowboy Atheist."

UPS saving millions on gas by routing their trucks to take mostly right-hand turns.

Rick Moody may or may not be the worst writer of his generation, but he is certainly not the worst *italicizer* of his generation.

"Time for bed little mouse little mouse. Today's median rating on the F.O.D. meter: 17.2."

How Jordan's childhood friend Avi, fifteen years to my eighteen, told me that one of the chief qualities of my personality is the quality of exaggeration. I believe his exact words were these: *Practically everything that comes out of your mouth is an exaggeration.*

If I die before I publish, I pray to a literary executor my book to take.

The audio track from the first 30 minutes of *Saving Private Ryan* swapped out with Megadeth's *Countdown to Extinction*.

The audio track from any of Spielberg's period films swapped out with an intermittent laugh track.

"No matter how drunk I get tonight I'll still have to go to work in the morning."

Character nightly revising his Last Will and Testament: "Didn't say a single word to me at the party tonight. Motherfucker just lost him a first-edition Pynchon."

Historically, the contradiction between my *manner of living*—e.g., snorting things off dirty tables in the back of Mexican pharmacies—and the near constancy of my debilitating *fear of death*.

Anymore my moments of mystical sublimity involve some variation on the following biological-determinist lamentation: I like to fuck because I am animal, not because I am human.

Republicans should stop going after rap and start going after Ligeti, for his is truly the devil's music.

In the evening, Carmen and I *bask in the pungency* of Jackson's feet after a day of his wearing shoes without socks.

How I used take care in what I said and thought for fear of not getting into heaven.

Life is not a joke—one only *wishes* it were.

Now that I have a wife and children I'll always have a selection of people to choose from upon whom I can blame my life's failures.

The best way to tackle the problem of death is to begin drinking early in the day.

What if I had to choose, under threat of losing one forever, between poetry and pornography?

To write that sort of first book of which people say, "He sure has fucked himself for the second book."

How often I've had a thought I felt *I must write down right away* and how often I've forgotten my thought between having it and finding a pen. It's as if I go through life in a permanent state of having awoken only seconds earlier, always trying and failing to remember my dreams.

Nietzsche, Kierkegaard and Wittgenstein are among my favorite philosophers if only because they are often very funny. All three perceive and articulate the inseparability—known to many but demonstrated by very few philosophers—of the tragic and the comic.

When reading a contemporary memoir, the exciting feeling that these people are actually *alive in the world.*

What if God had said to Phil Mickelson, *Would you rather shit your pants or shoot a double bogey on the 18th hole in the U.S. Open?*

Novel in which a young male protagonist is raised almost exclusively by his father. The boy's mother, suffering from a number of chronic illnesses, perpetually bed-ridden, absent. Mother's health eventually picks up enough to divorce father, who becomes resentful, often speaking disparagingly about mother to son, going even so far to suggest mother's illnesses *were a put-on*. Mother catches wind of father's behavior and retaliates, suggesting to son that father *needed mother to be sick all those years in order to get his rocks off playing God*, etc. First-person narrator, protagonist as adult, differentiates between real memories and memories as they've been influenced by vituperation of parents *ex post facto*, often offering three examples of the same memory—1) the event as influenced by the anger of the mother, 2) the event as influenced by the anger of the father, 3) the event as pieced together by the protagonist—leaving the choice, finally, up to the reader. A Choose-Your-Own-Recovered-Memory Novel.

Prose poem about a young boy burying things—toys, books, computer parts—in the backyard while his mother, at death's door, watches from the window.

"Nice shoes, Dada." "Nice boots, Dada." "Nice feep-fops, Dada."

Epic poem about someone reading *Finnegans Wake*.

Do I behave as if I'm the only pebble on the beach?

If I affix a single further accessory to Jackson's trike—another taillight, another high-candlepower LED, another flag, another horn or bell—only then might someone legitimately call the trike *gaudy*. As it is now, his trike is merely *well accessorized*.

Having forgotten whether or not I'd taken a Valium thirty seconds after having possibly taken one. Having forgotten whether or not I'd taken a second Valium thirty seconds after having possibly taken one to make up for possibly not having taken a first.

Having possibly shampooed my hair three times in a single showering.

Bumper sticker: "Don't Mess With Texas, Osama."

Being told as a child that if you write on your hand you'll get skin cancer.

Writing on my hand nearly every day now, taking my chances.

The word *nerdtacular*.

Ligeti adapting an etude for player piano and human: the human pianist sitting upon the bench of the player piano, watching the keys jump up and down, readying himself to reach in and play a chord, feeling that if he's not careful he'll get bitten.

To Carmen

    or:

In Token
of my admiration for his genius,
This book is inscribed
to
DAVID FOSTER WALLACE

    or:

For Mc.

In revision I'll have to tone down the self-masturbatoriness of F.O.N. if I hope to receive any positive reviews on it.

I say that I *fear death* or that I *have a problem with the fear of death* or that I *am constantly thinking about and fearing death*—but none of these is quite correct. Perhaps I don't fear *death* so much as I fear *life*: when I say *fear of death* what I really mean to say is *anxiety about the problem of life* vis-à-vis *the fact of death*.

At Wal-Mart today an elderly man in the adjacent urinal splashed his piss all over my flip-flopped feet.

How shortly after my brother learned to read I wrote the following words on a piece of paper and slid it beneath his bedroom door before he awoke one morning: I WILL KILL YOU JORDAN. How I waited in the hallway with great anticipation. How he finally opened the bedroom door to begin his day much later than usual.

Will Jackson develop an aversion to books because his father neglected him on their account? Nearly every day now he grabs a book from my hands and speaks angrily, "*Dada, stop reading!*"

Reading Nietzsche I sometimes feel the urge to leave my family, hop on a plane to a third-world country and have straight-up animal sex with as many peasant women as will have me.

The desert-island story, the *robinsonnade*, can be a means by which the author interrogates, negatively, the parameters of the social construction of identity.

Tom Hanks is spokesperson for Baby Boomer nostalgia.

"Allah! Buddha! Christ! Join forces just this once to help me find my goddamn cell phone!"

If my name had a *k* in it I could then count *knave* among its anagrams.

Love's Labor Won.

It's as if what we're getting in Ligeti's etudes performed by player piano is an extraterrestrial rendition of something composed by a human.

When Justin needed his birth certificate to obtain a driver's license, learning, to his astonishment, of his second middle name—Rupkin or Rufkin or Prufkin or something—the name being that of his mother's first husband, a suicide.

    I must be misremembering.

To journal is among my all-time least favorite verbs.

From Old Notebooks as the presentation of a subject through his daily jottings-down.

Top destination for wedding anniversary dinners in Las Cruces: Pizza Hut.

How, when we were kids, the calling of *shotgun* was a primary source of argumentation between Jordan and me.

In my writing until now I believe I have always striven first for *clarity of expression* and second for *clarity of thought*. But I know there is a threshold beyond which the distinction between *expression* and *thought* is no longer perceived as analogous to that of *form* and *content*, where thought itself is perceived as the precondition to this distinction, where form and content are revealed as *two forms of the same*: *thought*. (So I suppose form still prevails, in any case.) This may be the trump card philosophy holds over poetry: Thought *subsumes* its own expression. But then again, philosophy is *written*—isn't it?

It hurts to wear my baseball glove with my wedding ring on.

I can translate the word *life* into two other languages off the top of my head, the word *death* into five.

The pocket protector, signet of self-nerdification.
   Must get one.

From Old Notebooks: A Showing-Off.

How maybe half of the sentences in *Infinite Jest* contain humor in consequence of self-consciously awkward prose.
   Wallace's may be the geekiest prose in the history of literature.

The increased widespread anxiety of near apocalypse is symptom to the tyranny of the image. We're worried that the world could end at any moment—on TV.

I often—very often, in fact—*pretend* to be going poo, in order to have a moment of privacy from my family.

"Jackson, do you love your Grandpa?"
   "Much."
   "Do you love your Grandma?"

"Much."

"Do you love your Uncle Jordan?"

"Much."

"Do you love your Mama?"

"Much."

"Do you love Sequoia?"

"Much."

"Do you love this dust mote?"

"Much."

From Old Notebooks: One Thanataphobe's Journey.

I worry about awaking from some sort of high-tech hibernant state to a distant future in which everyone is far advanced of me, is laughing at me; in which my knowledge of the world is entirely obsolete.

When reading an anthology of Beckett's work arranged in chronological order, always start from the back.

To live along the white creases inside Sofia's elbows, the backsides of her knees and knuckles.

The world is everything that is the case.

The world is everything that is not the case. The world is nothing that is the case.

The world is everything and nothing that is and is not the case.

Terrible premonition of our upcoming road trip to visit Dad: jackknifed by a semi, turn back to see Jackson's head hanging.

Have written it—nothing can happen.

How I've always felt so sure I would someday lose or mangle my fingers in a garbage disposal.

How I've always felt sure I would die of electrocution while standing in a puddle of milk. Or die in a car recently fallen from a cliff.

Using the occasion of F.O.N. to catalog all my problems.

After a man/woman undergoes sexual reassignment surgery, for what length of time does the passing of the public bathroom designated for the sexual category opposite to his/her post-op category constitute an *event* for this person?

Nearly having an accident when swerving over to the side of the road to write down an idea.

The *buoyancy* of Carmen's voice: I am lifted from the dregs of self-absorption and carried into the world.

A giant meteor striking and obliterating Earth, casting the entire body of Shakespeare's work into oblivion.

Not to mention the entire human race.

The one recurring nightmare I've had in my life involves my mother's voice calling out to me from a house made of shattered black glass. Hers is at once the most familiar voice, and the strangest. Do I follow the voice, toward the shattered house? Or do I flee for my life?

A Portrait of the Artist as a Young Father.

Why do philosophers always strive for consistency? A philosophy that is everywhere contradictory would better correspond to the world it describes. Philosophy is a slave—a stalker—to science and scientific thinking, in this respect.

How writing seems to me the most egocentric of all acts, no matter which way you cut it, de Sade or Solzhenitsyn.

I often worry I will *suddenly remember* that I am supposed to be taking care of Jackson or Sofia.

Is there a moment in *Ulysses* when in interior monologue the thinking character needlessly worries that someone physically proximate might overhear his thoughts? I needlessly worry that people will overhear my thoughts all the time.

Hearing a pianist play a piece of music one has grown accustomed to hearing played by a different pianist can be either exhilarating or disappointing, very much like the experience of kissing someone for the first time.

The anxiety I felt as a teenager about not having enough wet dreams, an anxiety I sometimes still feel.

How my last resort when arguing with Carmen about needing more time to read and write is to threaten divorce.

When driving on a highway through unpopulated areas, the feeling that one could pull over to the shoulder, hop over the barbed wire fence, run perpendicular to the highway for ten minutes and end up standing on a patch of ground where no one has ever stood before.

Driving on: "Anyhow, I'm sure someone has stood there before."

Whenever I am despairing of existence, here is the thought that will sometimes get me through: *At least I can always go back and re-read Melville's early novels.*

The book as a *closed system*, containing all possible interpretation of itself. How would such a book be read? Why would anyone want to read such a thing?

The scientist to the philosopher: "Get over yourself."

The philosopher to the scientist: "~~Get over your world~~."

It is often said of the families in horror films of the *Poltergeist* ilk, *The idiots should have moved away*. However, were I to suspect the presence of the supernatural in my own house, I would investigate the matter thoroughly, staying as long as needed to either scientifically deny the existence of the ghosts and thus confirm my nonbelief, or scientifically confirm the existence of the ghosts and finally deny my nonbelief. If ever an opportunity arises by which there exists even the slightest, even the most unlikely possibility of my glimpsing the supernatural—even if I am 99% sure the sound I hear in the middle of the night is the expanding fir of the ceiling joists—I should be ever eager to throw on my deerstalker cap and wipe clean my magnifying glass.

Dad: "I'm going to wear overalls in retirement."

"To his interviewer's query concerning the single characteristic shared by all his life's work, the aged author replied, 'Bullshit.'"

Without porn for a week. Longest stretch since childhood.

In reply to Dad telling me that I am a good father: "I learned from the master."

The headlights passing on the interstate: the momentary gazes of countless strangers.

The pleasure of philosophy involves the reader's inhabitation of a shared space of abstract thought—the book.

A stoner driving west could experience two *4:20*s in the same day.

"Dump twuck." "Cah carryuh." "Pick-up twuck." "Digga." "Mobile kwane." "Fwunt woaduh." "Fiuh twuck." "Giant escavatuh." "Cement mixuh." "Monsta twuck." "Moving twuck."

To make enough money to be able to purchase a desk and a chair and rent a small room or closet in which I can position the height of the chair in relation to the desk such that typing will not result in this horrible ache in my wrists.

Footage of United 175 impacting WTC South v. footage of U.S. Engineer Eugene Armstrong decapitated.

When I was a child I thought of death as choice, not inevitability. As if all those who died had simply been weak of will.
    Sometimes I still believe that.

Don't apologize for the aphorism by substituting *I* for *one*—that is a retreat from faith.

Three things I would try my hardest to save were my house on fire: flash drive, baseball glove, first-edition *Gravity's Rainbow*.

Three more: Carmen, Jackson, Sofia.

From Old Notebooks: A Preface.

West of El Paso, a billboard advertisement for a local hospital depicts a cute Latino toddler next to these words: *Is He Yours? Be Sure.*

As a child I was told by a teacher that if the largest telescope on Earth were placed on Mars and turned toward Earth the only visible trace of life would be all the millions of slowly moving roofs of automobiles.

Evan Lavender-Smith, of Las Cruces, a part-time college instructor, died Sunday at Memorial Medical Center. He was 82. Mr. Lavender-Smith died of excessive masturbation.

Born September 6, 1977, in Des Moines, IA, he was the son of the late Barry Smith and Gail Lavender.

Mr. Lavender-Smith taught introductory composition and technical writing at New Mexico State University for 58 years. His writing appeared in *Colorado Review*, *Denver Quarterly* and *Land-Grant College Review*. He self-published a book entitled *From Old Notebooks* in 2032.

He is survived by a son, Jackson Smith, of Paris, France; a daughter, Sofia Smith, of London; a wife, Carmen Smith, of Las Cruces; a brother, Jordan Lavender-Smith, of New York City; as well as seven grandchildren and eighteen great-grandchildren.

F.O.N. as the prelude to a larger body of work. F.O.N. as everywhere self-consciously introductory.

I am tempted to cut out that patch of skin from Sofia's back containing her birthmark—crimson relief of Kauai—before it fades any further.

The question *Why is there something rather than nothing?* can originate only in the context of mortality.

How Jordan refers to masturbating as *doing it to yourself*. E.g., "Make sure to knock when the shutters are down because I might be in there *doing it to myself*." "Evan, did you fall in or are you in there *doing it to yourself*?"

How I was brought in as a reliever in the Las Cruces Little League Championship and called for a balk before throwing my first pitch.

The book as notes toward the composition of the book . . . ?

One might say that the structure of *Being and Time* is beautiful insofar as it is designed, in its totality, to broach a single question.

Off on safari in the knotted jungle of Jackson's hair.

To retrieve my MFA thesis from the stacks, take it with me into the third-floor bathroom stall, tear out the pages and flush them down.

From Old Notebooks: A Record of Youth's Folly.

I count David Markson's literary-anecdote books among the few things I want to read over and over again, yet I have no idea whether they are actually any good. They're like porn for English majors.

Despite the august pride we felt as children reciting the "Pledge of Allegiance" or singing "The Star-Spangled Banner," it is extremely doubtful that we will encourage our children to be proud Americans.

The existence of God is as obvious as the flatness of the Earth.

Televised sports have taken on new importance in my life since having children.

How nice it would be if F.O.N. progressed toward a *coming-down-from-the-citadel.*

Do other people think about death as much as I do?

I've asked the question of a number of people—"Are you concerned with the fact that you're going to die someday? And does this knowledge not weigh on you so heavily?"—and the most common response has been, "What the hell are you talking about?"

Only after opening one's seventh Miller High Life of the evening can one honestly say it tastes like champagne.

"I have just now arrived at the solution to the greatest theoretical problem faced by 20th-century aestheticians, that of distinguishing poetic language and ordinary language. Here it is: *You are all a bunch of snobs!*"

"Dada, fix it."

It is a frightening thought that philosophy has always and will always continue to fall within the purview of science and scientific thinking. The philosopher who insists he is operating outside the purview of science is much like the toddler with diarrhea running down his legs who insists he does not have a dirty diaper.

Should I be concerned about *exploiting my children* by including them in F.O.N?

As a teenager I asked Mc, "How can someone as smart as you be so devoutly religious?"

His reply: "Religion is my absurd struggle. We all need one."

How, the summer we mowed lawns for money, Justin and I drove across town wearing our white dust masks. How a homeless man approached us at an intersection to shout, *That's right! Don't breathe the air, man!* How we nonchalantly lifted the burning cigarettes from the truck's ashtray, placed their filters against our dust masks, inhaled. How the homeless man's laughter convulsed and convulsed.

Visit Zuhl Library at New Mexico State University, Southwestern New Mexico's Most Comprehensive Collection of Petrified Wood.

From Old Notebooks: A Novel: An Essay.
    From Old Notebooks: An Essay: A Novel.

Living in mourning thereof.

Jackson's ear fetish—his ultimate display of affection is to roll a person's earlobe between his fingers—has found its fixation permanently fulfilled in Sofia's elfin ears. I often come upon them in Jackson's room, his arms reaching out to either side of her head, his half-open mouth, his concentrated eyes, busy fingers. . . . Sofia's expression is one of bewildered concession, and that's when she looks the most like her mother: it's the same facial expression on Carmen with which I'm most familiar.

Am I eager to classify F.O.N. as a novel because I want to avoid admitting that any of it is true? What is said at one point might have been true at the time but may not be true later in the book, may not be true now. Truth, in the world of the book, is instantaneous; it has no duration. Fifty entries from now, I might write, "Truth, in the world of the book, is not instantaneous; it has duration."

Graffitied spread-eagled woman on inside of bathroom stall: *Invitation to masturbate?*

Upon first meeting the parents of someone you've known for a long time and noticing bits and pieces of her face in the faces of her parents.

Is the elevated syntax of F.O.N. a syntax of avoidance?

I am less mindful of the contrivance of the *monologue intérieur* because with each subsequent reading of *Ulysses* my own thoughts are proceeding that much more in the manner of the contrivance.

Sometimes Jackson's diaper is so stinky it seems as if he must have eaten shit instead of food and what I'm dealing with here is not regular shit but shit squared.

How the decline of my once-keen mathematical skills may be attributable to the slaphappiness with which I reach for my fancy graphing calculator.

It seems that the history of philosophy proceeds like this: Philosopher 1 posits Z, Philosopher 2 comes along and says, *Yes, I understand perfectly well why you would have mistakenly posited Z—it is because you have failed to consider Y*, Philosopher 3 comes along and tells 2 that he has failed to consider X, Philosopher 4 tells 3 he has failed to consider W, so on and so forth. The carrot dangling before the nose of philosophy is the carrot of the A.

Carmen and I are off on another shit hunt. We move stealthily from room to room, guided only by our noses. We will eventually root out the shit, and we will destroy it.

A Portrait of the Solipsist as a Young Father.

Did DeLillo think we wouldn't notice all the recycled material in *Game 6–Cosmopolis*? Does he not care?

Is he not supposed to care?

The political situation in America has, for many of us, re-invigorated the question of God: we feel that God has risen from his grave only to put on a power suit, so we've decided to re-believe in God in order to create an oppositional God, a Birkenstocked God.

Were my life cut short, were I to die today, could it be said I was *ready to die*?

Hell to the nah.

1 can Red Bull + 2.5 oz. vodka.

750 ml. vodka = 25 oz. vodka.

Buy 10 cans Red Bull.

Carmen's voice beckons from the bathroom—"*No TP!*"—and at last I am put to some real use in the world.

The American counteroffensive to terrorist bombings is longer lines at airport security checkpoints.

There was, when I was young, a depth to everything at Disneyland, an imaginary narrative or history to every object, worlds now barely perceptible.

Bildingsroman, schmildingsfauxpawn.

"In order to become seriously religious I'm going to have to undo 28 years of honing my skills at the detection of bullshit."

The word *essay* used to describe that formally daring writing once described by the word *novel*.

Disneyland is shielded from cultural criticism. By what? By Disneyland.

Today I have heard and absorbed your theories, Disneyland says, and tonight I will explode them in my light show.

Interviewer: "So if you aren't willing to discuss your book, what is it you are willing to discuss?"

Queasy, overcandied Jackson's vomit is held at bay somewhere in his legs, he insists.

Disneyland, The Melancholiest Place on Earth.

The first word of *Ulysses* as grammatical analogue to Rubin's vase–profile illusion: half the time I read it it's an adjective, the other half an adverb.

One book. Two planes.

CNN in the cockpit so the pilot knows with what tone to address the passengers.

There is no chain of signification when lightning strikes.

In my next life I would like to be an astronomer.

When I've reached that point at which I no longer fear going naked in public, I imagine I will also have reached the point at which I'm no longer consumed by F.O.D. That is to say, never.

Whether or not we are able to surface from the cynicism of our late youth will determine the spiritual tenor of the rest of our lives.

What prevents the author of *De la grammatologie* from appending his name to the book like this: ~~Jacques Derrida~~? Or the author of *From Old Notebooks* appending his name like this: ~~Evan Lavender-Smith~~? The physical book itself suggests a certain stability, perhaps, stable subject, stable sign. Perhaps it would be helpful if books were printed on tissue paper or on sand.

Dada farts.

 Dada: "Jackson, you farted!"

 Jackson: "No, Dada farted."

 Mama farts.

 Mama: "Jackson, you farted!"

 Jackson: "No, Mama farted."

 Baby Sista farts.

 Dada: "Jackson, you farted!"

 Jackson: "No, Baby Sista farted."

 Jackson farts.

 Dada: "Who farted?"

 Long pause.

Perhaps there is nothing quintessentially postmodern about the self-reflexivity, fragmentation and pastiche of F.O.N., if only because all of it follows from form.

Too often taking a joke one step too far: Justin's observation that all our furniture is crammed into one corner of the dining room—my suggestion that I should serve small portions of food on one corner of the plate—followed by my suggestion that I should serve dinner wearing only one-fourth of a T-shirt.

Does the type of flooring present in the house in which one grew up factor in any quantifiable way into one's psychological development?

As an accurate record of my life as a parent, this book doesn't hold a candle to *my shirt*—old poo stains and spaghetti stains and vomit stains and mustard stains, old apocryphal stains . . . My shit-stained wardrobe, my *oeuvre*.

I hate all films—with many exceptions.

Here are the side effects I experience when starting Wellbutrin, so to not freak out the next time I start: headaches, premature ejaculation, increased morbid thoughts, increased susceptibility to caffeine addiction, nausea, insomnia, dizziness, increased spacing-out, bubbling and twitching in eyebrows and forehead, heartburn, high-pitched ringing in ears, attention span difficulties, earaches, dry mouth, jaw aches, and grinding of teeth.

I get jealous when playing catch with someone whose baseball glove is more worn out than mine.

To Sofia, at the age of four months, my words are neither meaningful nor meaningless—there is simply no question of meaning.

When activities ancillary to being a poet—teaching, attending conferences, giving readings, publishing—become primary, the poet becomes professional, a professional poet, a *pro-po*. Here is the signifying chain corresponding to *contemporary American poetry*: go to party, give reading, attend conference, teach, go to party, attend conference, judge contest, give reading, go to party, teach, judge contest, attend conference . . .

The relationship of the events as they occurred in the time of my life to the manner in which those events are depicted *at a remove* in the time of the book might best be described in metaphor: prism? carpenter's scribe? seismograph?

"I sometimes suspect I might be the most narcissistic person in the world—not only among the living, but among all the dead. The most narcissistic person in human history." Pause. "Or at the very least tied for first."

How I can grow angered with people for their behavior in my reveries, e.g., Mom never willing to give up her life for Jackson's when the armed intruder has a gun to both their heads.

Are Martha Clifford and Nurse Callan the same person? What is "U.p:up"? Who is the Man in the Macintosh?

It wouldn't surprise me to learn that companies I associate only with home appliance manufacture make very different things in other countries: A pick-up truck in Japan might have the Frigidaire logo on its tailgate.

Likewise, if we were to locate an advanced civilization on a distant planet and travel there to visit, it should not surprise us to learn that nearly every city block contains a Starbucks.

Our attitude toward the mystery of death when we were kids: *We'll get to the bottom of this soon enough!*

When doing the dishes first thing in the morning, I feel that if the conditions of my life were altered slightly—for instance, if we had three children instead of two, or if I were missing an arm—I could find myself in a situation where I would have to spend the entirety of the day doing dishes in order to keep up with the dirty dishes coming in—which day might in fact turn out to be a very *happy day*, a day during which I think very little about *death*.

I become so spaced-out when doing the dishes such that a full five minutes might elapse between the rinsing of one dish and the next, during which time I might stare ahead blankly; or I will load the dishwasher and immediately thereafter unload it, without having run it, and shelve all those dirty dishes.

It's surprising that I don't often leave the house wearing my shoes and socks on my hands.

We let go of the atheism of our youth not because we grow wiser but because the thought of atheism becomes more and more difficult to maintain.

There is a palette of colors ranging from soot black to chamois from which God selects one, at his fancy, to hue Jackson's poo.

"Do you think we should leave Iraq now?"

All the thousands of people across the country dashing to their telephones to be charged for an opinion based on his or her political dogmatism combined with a negligible admixture of all the worthless information gleaned from watching CNN.

Being is a bump along the smooth surface of non-being.

Does everyone have a facial expression he or she automatically puts on when looking in the mirror, or is it just me?

I have no idea what my real face looks like. In my third-person dreams I wear my mirror face at all times: eyes squinted, lips smirked, eyebrows arched like Jack Nicholson's.

I never *felt* the project of ontology until taking Zoloft. Zoloft *activated* ontology for me.

I am *bludgeoning* Jackson with ostensive definitions of color in order to try to get him to understand color as distinct from concepts like shape and size. I seem to bludgeon him especially with definitions of the color red, if only because there always seems to be a toy fire truck close at hand.

Philosophers say that we are bound by the limits imposed by language or being or structure—that we are *stuck* and must work or play within these limits, that we must, as the sage says, *Make it work.*

Is a philosophy of unstuckedness necessarily a theology? No—it is a necessarily a book.

From Old Notebooks: A Memoivel in Verse with Philosophical Flourishes.

Jackson, pointing at a moth fluttering by: "A life! A life!"

God endowed the universe with an infinite number of signs, but only one fact.

The image of beauty that would instantly dispel all doubt—Jackson taking a bath, Carmen raising two fingers to her lips, empty autumn baseball field—for which I am constantly on the lookout and never able to quite resolve.

If I were a painter, what would my paintings look like?

Wellbutrin babies.

"Oh, hadn't you heard? The problem of life and death was solved last year by a team of physicists in Hamburg. There's absolutely nothing to worry about anymore."

That v. *which*.

What Bloom almost wrote in the sand: I AM A CUCKOLD.
  I AM ALONE.
  I AM A FOOL.
  I AM A NAUGHTY BOY.
  "I AM A _____: What Bloom Almost Wrote in the Sand."

Death, in F.O.N., is even a matter of form, the posthumous collection of jottings-down.

To overcome the problem of life and death, one must either *sacrifice the intellect*, per Pascal, or *forget*, per Nietzsche. Since we've been trained since childhood to do both, per TV, the problem of life and death really shouldn't pose much of a problem for this generation.

Sometimes when on the internet I'll accidentally click my way to bona fide child pornography.

I never include the date above anything I write, an act of defiance I commit against my literary executors.

"If I can just keep up this level of caffeine intake for a little while longer, literary fame will surely follow."

From Old Notebooks: Solipsism's End.

Last thing Jackson said before falling asleep last night: "Dada, my need pee-bee-and-jay."

First thing he said upon waking this morning, ten hours later: "Dada, my need pee-bee-and-jay."

That the assumptions philosophers question are the same assumptions which have led to the unprecedented flourishing of a species—that is only a slight snag, and is, besides, a very *provincial* thing to say.

I understand so little of the great late-20th-century poetry. There is no novel of the late 20th century I have yet encountered, or any book of philosophy or literary theory or linguistics that is to me unapproachable in the way of a small volume of poems by John Ashbery. What in the world is wrong with me?

As for the more conservative strains of late-20th-century poetry, that is poetry I can *really understand*, poetry I can *really hate*.

How much I regret those years during which I chose downers over uppers.

Is Carmen truly not desirous of immortality or is she just letting on to reveal the pettiness of my desire?

Death is the glue that holds the book together.

For the theoretical physicist of this century, the hypothesis of infinite time should at once contain and not contain God.

When I say that I *love* Jackson, or I *love* Carmen or Sofia, to what extent is this love culturally conditioned? The biological condition is clear enough—love is a trick of biology; love is my symptom—but in recent history, have fathers always *loved* their sons as I love Jackson? Love circa 2000 B.C. versus love circa 2000 A.D: Certainly it would not occur to me to *lovingly* send Jackson off to war, yet that may have much less to do with culture than one imagines.

Or has paternal love changed only relative to the constancy of maternal love? The passion with which mothers have attempted to prevent their sons from going to war, I don't imagine that passion has *increased* over the past few thousand years. Unlike paternal love, we never think of it as a matter of *degree* with maternal love.

—Except for with my mother.

"Important world events are all happening over there, on the other side of an ocean. When I think of something happening over here, I get scared, but I also get really excited."

We're anxious for *our turn*, because *we never* get to play.

Carmen and I have very few opportunities for sex, and often resort to having sex with Sofia on the bed with us, sometimes asleep, more often than not awake, breastfeeding, watching.

Not exactly the *ménage à trois* I had always hoped for.

In a certain respect, F.O.N. represents little more than the garbage can of my imagination.

A good dedication page for a book in which the clock is really ticking: *I have plenty of people to thank but there's no time for that now . . . to you, to me, to the book—*

If only I keep writing about death, maybe it will go away.

Justin's dad's friend, a theoretical physicist who kept a copy of his own book in his breast pocket to quote from when someone put to him a difficult question of theoretical physics.

De vieux cahiers. Aus alten Heften. De los Cuadernos Viejos.

I never read the books from my reading stack but always reach beyond the stack to retrieve a book from the shelf. After reading the book from the shelf, the stack is outmoded. I reshelve the stack and start a new stack that I will not read from.

I use the words *tenuous* and *precarious* to describe what might better be described as the *delicate* or the *fragile* state of my consciousness, as opposed to that *hardy* or *rugged* state entirely foreign to me yet very possibly the *status quo*.

How we used to *sham for shotgun*.

F.O.N. presents a subject wearing only the tatters of language.

I can imagine F.O.N. following Kierkegaard's method of *indirect* communication, but hopefully with less rhetoric. I can imagine the book as performative philosophy, or anti-philosophy, or improvisational philosophy (or—*gulp*—pseudo-philosophy).

My fear of death and my habit of not looking people in the eyes when I speak are related, I'm sure.

Whenever I start taking Wellbutrin again that precious *I* loses a little more determinacy.

I have a specific, corporeal sensation associated with my memory of reading Deleuze, as I have of reading Cormac McCarthy, of DeLillo, of Pynchon, and many others. Attempting to pin down the sensation is much like attempting to pin down the elusive mnemonic referent to a smell that evokes seemingly strong and particular yet decontexualized and fleeting and finally obscure sense memory. Trying to wrap my mind around the sensation leaves me *flustered*, and attempting to *think* the sensation *defeats* it.

Perhaps the Deleuzian reading sensation or the Pynchonian reading sensation follows from a memory composed of a complex of rhythms (syntactical rhythms, tonal rhythms, structural rhythms) specific to my reading of that author's books, which may or may not correspond to the complex of rhythms specific to a human consciousness (or a collision of two consciousnesses). Although it now seems the sensation could have as much to do with rhythm as with the type of paper the words are printed on, or the typeface, or even the smell of the book. I would be wise to leave it alone, to say of it, *What a pleasant mystery*, but instead I must murder it.

I cannot leave the house without wearing a belt, no matter how snugly my pants fit.

I have read the great poetry that is no fun to read, but not the great novel.

While my thoughts are not quite as sharp on Wellbutrin, they are more plentiful: compose while on Wellbutrin, revise while not.

If we are as proximate to Bloom's consciousness as we think we are, we should be able to complete his sentence in the sand, but we cannot: Joyce is phasing him out.

In a sea of eternity one would eternally drown and eternally surface.

She walks from room to room in F.O.N. to find everything perfectly normal, but when she descends to the basement, a gap in the drywall reveals that the house has been framed with synthetic wood.

It would seem I experience time somewhat differently on Wellbutrin: my days now feel as if they contain maybe 26 hours.

"My fear of death is much more well formed than anybody else's. *Your fear of death is* nothing *compared to mine.*"

The satisfaction Carmen takes in paying for things with pennies, nickels and dimes.

Some of the world's finest detectives may work in the field of sprinkler-system repair.

Whenever I start taking Wellbutrin again I think an awful lot about the fact of my being on it, and I'm eager to talk to other people, even strangers, about my being on it. All drugs can be like this to some extent, some more than others.

"Dada, what the heck?"

From Old Notebooks might reflect nature in its condition of false unmolestation.

If not nicotine, alcohol. If not alcohol, caffeine. If not caffeine, Xanax. If not Xanax, Valium. If not Valium, nicotine.

Does it often happen that protégés unconsciously emulate the handwriting of their mentors, as I have Mc's?

A reader could make a case that there are a number of *elided texts* within or suggested by *From Old Notebooks*, including the one that gives the author the authority to write such a book.

The word *shebeenkeeper*.

A great work of art that does not aspire to greatness.

Are the dreams of people of greater intelligence easier or harder to interpret than those of lesser intelligence? Are the dreams of the artist any more or less beautiful than the dreams of the idiot?

"Did you ever consider the possibility that death might not be the end?"
"No."

It would be better if we all began pronouncing the word *science* as it is pronounced as the root in *conscience*, thus: "shints."
E.g., "He is debating whether to devote his life to the study of religion or the study of ['shints']."

There are certain smells that have the power to dissolve the problem of life.

The opposite of *desiring something more of life* is either *desiring nothing more of life* or *desiring something less of life*.

The smell of Sofia's head sweat.

From Old Notebooks: A Cry for Help.

It seems to me that evolution has proceeded one step too far with respect to the survival and dominance of a species of organisms cognizant of their own mortality.

Evolution, too, has entered the Age of Irony.

Dream last night of a volleyball match between the Happies and the Sads to determine the future course of western literature.

The method of Sigmund Freud is similar to the method of Sherlock Holmes: highly improbable and highly entertaining.

Art *sans* artifice.

At the moment I imagine F.O.N. to be barely yet necessarily a novel.

Sometimes it seems like I'm really reading when I'm writing and really writing when I'm reading.

"Since I'll never have a chance to grieve the loss of my own life, that's what I'll spend my life doing."

Is Joyce's sexism pardonable?

The question of being is more accessible on a cloudy day.

The difference between drinking Pepsi and Diet Pepsi is for me the difference between practicing total abandon and total restraint.

If David Markson hadn't written his literary-anecdote novels, would I have ever thought to consider F.O.N. a novel? Would I have ever thought to write such a book?

O kind Wellbutrin! O good-natured Zoloft! O rosy-fingered Zantac 150!

Mornings my brain is a wet sponge, wrung out by writing before noon.

"Dada, what's that?"
    "That's a straw."
    "Why?"

For fear of total embarrassment, covering my ears at the drive-thru lane with Carmen and Rachel.

It is unfortunate that philosophy-meets-fiction finds its popular contemporary examples in works like those of Robert Pirsig, because such books do justice to neither the philosophy nor the fiction: each feels watered down, and an imposition on the other. What is needed are books in which distinctions such as philosophy/fiction or poetry/fiction or fiction/nonfiction are not enacted, but everywhere made immediately irrelevant.

When I was a kid I thought that mono was caused by excessive kissing.

It is so glaringly obvious that the dead rat I found in the yard today has not moved on to *something else*.

Collage in F.O.N. is incidental to form. The input of the book is chronology and the output is collage.

I can imagine translating a book from one language to another as an act of thanksgiving.

Joycespeare.

Now that I've cut my hair from a uniform length of ½" to ¼", my brain feels twice as exposed to the elements.

Is internet porn responsible for the decreasing population of so many countries?

The modern sensibility is a hyperbolic sensibility. —Or is it just mine?

Being and God are two sides of the same coin. We atheists insist on keeping the coin face down at all times.

The self-reflexivity in F.O.N. is in earnest, I hope.

After studying it for more than twenty years, the evening sky in New Mexico is still no less strange than my strangest hallucination.

Mom coming to the house the day Sofia was born, helping me clean the vernix from her, giving her a cursory—grandmotherly—head-to-toe physical exam. Saying of her grand-daughter's vulva, "Now that doesn't look right. You'll need to have that checked out right away." My heart stopping. The wheels in Mom's mind turning: "But of course as a mother of two boys I don't know a thing about little girls' anatomies."

Mom coming to the house to play with Jackson, asking permission to enroll him in a yoga class for toddlers: "Last week I noticed he's only using one side of his body. One whole side of him isn't active. As if one side of him is slightly paralyzed. His left side, I think." My heart stopping. Mom playing with him a while, calling out from his room, "Forget that yoga class idea! Both sides of his body are working great!"

Intellectuals Anonymous.

The thought that my fear of death might one day pass was, in my teens, a cause of unrest and concern: *Let's not forget this feeling! Let's never give up, never give in! Let's be mad at death forever!*

The thought that my fear of death might one day pass is, in my late twenties, immeasurably comforting: *Anything to get rid of this feeling! I give up, I give in! Let's be OK with death forever!*

I would be very envious to meet a great artist who had the strength of will not to create any art.

Carmen is the *best* person I have ever known, perforce the *silliest* person.

Art is the invitation to a worldview.

"When I see on television that some catastrophe has happened somewhere in the world my first impulse is to make a bowl of popcorn."

Regis: "And, for one million dollars . . . What type of cheese does Leopold Bloom ask for on the sandwich he orders for lunch in James Joyce's *Ulysses*?"
Evan: "Gorgonmotherfuckingzola!"

There may be a way to read F.O.N. by which entries that acknowledge the existence of the book—self-reflexive entries such as this one—are perceived as an imposition on the form of the book.
Is it necessary to say that I am composing this entry in the same breath that I am composing this entry? That I am writing the book while writing the book?

fauxPod is to iPod as WackBerry is to BlackBerry.

Although the contrivance of the linguistic fluidity of thought—the *lingualization of thought*—in *Ulysses* continues to bother me, the book remains among my all-time favorites because it is very boldly determined to demonstrate *the beauty* of thought.

What is required of a *successful younger poet* nowadays is a cursory understanding of 20th-century literary theory combined with a passing interest in language and grammar—also a tattoo will help.

"With your right hand grip a fistful of Baby Sister's onesie, with your left brace her head against your breast—we're going in for a crash landing."

There's no two ways about it, I am wasting my life on death.

When in the morning I attempt to recall my dreams and in doing recall a dream I dreamed many weeks or months earlier *and it is actually a dream from earlier that night.*

Learning today that terrorists were planning to blow up airplanes with Gatorade and iPods, it should become obvious that soon it will not be possible to stop terrorist attacks against airplanes short of banning humans from the planes.

The false assumption that in order to say anything meaningful one must know *all the rules of the game*—by extension, that nothing meaningful can be said—has discouraged at least one generation from attempting to say anything at all that could in the least be perceived as *naïve*.

"Jackson, how doing?" "Jackson, what doing?"

If ever there was a book destined for vanity publication, this is it.

It's hard to take Schopenhauer very seriously, because he's very angry, and so much of what we say when we're angry is nonsense.

When on ESPN we hear a commentator say, "It's only a game," we can't help but fidget. It's tantamount to the pastor of a church saying, "Life is not serious."

Makes breakfast for his wife. Goes to the butcher. Goes to the post office. Goes to a church. Goes to a chemist. Goes to a public bath. Goes to a funeral. Goes to a newspaper press. Goes to a locksmith to canvass an ad. Feeds some seagulls. Goes to a bar. Helps a blind man cross the street. Goes to the museum. Goes to the library. Visits a bookseller. Window-shops. Goes to a restaurant. Listens to some live music. Writes a love letter. Goes to another bar. Nearly gets in a fight. Masturbates to a beautiful eighteen-year-old exhibitionist giving him a private show. Takes an alfresco nap. Takes up a collection for a widow. Goes to a hospital to visit a pregnant woman. Flirts with a nurse. Feeds a stray dog. Goes to a whorehouse. Helps avert a row with the police. Goes to a cabman's shelter and listens to a sailor tell stories. Breaks into his own house. Urinates under the stars with another man. Watches the sunrise. Kisses his wife on her arse.

It would have been the single busiest, most adventurous day of my life.

All one really needs to be happy in life is a single other person to whom one may comfortably put such questions as *Does this hurt or feel good?* and *What is your most vivid memory of a thought you've had in the past?* and *Will you please describe the genitalia of every person you've had sexual intercourse with?*

How Carmen can recite most of the movie *Friday* from memory.

Ethics and ontology are inextricably bound in Heidegger. One must *earn* ontology in Heidegger. Heidegger enacts the *drama* of ontology.

I walk through life in a sort of daze that grows stronger by the semester.

In writing F.O.N. I have perhaps painted myself into a corner with respect to the next book; I feel as if I'm already writing in my *terminal style*. But that's how it should feel with every book, shouldn't it?

Or perhaps it's only that I will die soon.

F.O.D. may be symptom to my control-freakishness.

When Sofia and Jackson fall asleep in their car seats, we park the car in the garage and shut off the engine; they wake up half an hour later with their hair and shirts soaked in sweat. I hold them to feel the tack of wet against my skin, my cheek, my lips, and, when Carmen isn't looking, my tongue. Their sweat is not from concentrate, 100% pure real life.

Watching Carell's character teased mercilessly for his virginity in *The 40-Year-Old Virgin*, I think to myself, *How entirely foreign to my experience*, and seconds later recall an experience at summer camp when I was teased mercilessly for my virginity.

Schopenhauer has a Kant complex: he's mad at people who love Kant, he's mad at people who don't love Kant, he's mad at people who don't know Kant, and he's mad at Kant.

One of the saddest things about Dad having moved away is that there's no chance of accidentally running into him around campus anymore.

When I walk past a shop and catch a scent which sends me careening into the empty memory vortex, that I am learning new scents today which will send me careening there in the future.

These young female students do not have severe *outties*, it is simply that they have piercings in their navels which are creating bumps on their shirts.

People say Husserl is outmoded, but they would never say Kafka is outmoded. We say, "I need to read Husserl in order to understand Derrida," or "I need to read Bergson in order to understand Deleuze," but how often do we say, "I need to read Kafka in order to understand Brian Evenson"? Every philosophy contains the seed of its own obsolescence. *"All philosophical questioning is necessarily untimely"*: What Heidegger is saying without knowing it is, "All philosophy is doomed to obsolescence, to historical curiosity."

Every day billions of people literally pray to a figurative being. No wonder everyone thinks they're a poet.

That the solution to the problem of life is obvious and only *seemingly* counterintuitive: not to look inward but to look outward, to immerse myself in the worlds of other human beings.

But why is this so difficult to *realize*?

How readily I allow strange new verbs into my life—*to Tivo, to Google, to Ferberize*—as if I were some sort of linguistic slut.

My life is an unbroken chain of dreams to the occasional half-lucid jottings-down of F.O.N.

"The ATM *ate* my card." "The Coke machine *ate* my money."

It may not be fair to say that Wittgenstein wished he had been born a dog, but that can't be very far off the mark. I would imagine he thought of dogs and cats and other animals of a certain intermediate intelligence as *charmed*.

"There's no way I'm sticking my flash drive in that."

A problem with Shakespeare is that the contrast between innovation of language and derivativeness of plot is not *put to good use*, which often results in plot functioning merely as *an excuse* for language.

The book *reflects* a life.
    The book *refracts* a life.

The mistaken presupposition that the beauty of life precludes life's meaninglessness.

The syntax of the life remains the syntax of the book, but the stuff that proceeds syntax in life—the events of life—has been displaced by the *form* of the book (by the *sufficiency of the form*). Just as it is with language and music.

The artist is nearsighted: from afar the possibilities of his art are many, from anear they are one.

I have *perfected* my lecture after giving it for the third time, but my fourth class never gets to realize it because my voice is hoarse and I'm so tired from giving the same lecture four times in one day, so their experience of my perfect lecture at 8–9:40 PM is of approximately equal value to that of my students receiving my imperfect lecture at 8–9:40 AM, as well as my students at 2:30–3:55 and 5:30–7:10—and it all evens out to uniform mediocrity in the end.

Ideally, I would have one day to prepare a lecture for the following day, on which day I would give the lecture one time only.

Her mom refers to Carmen's pinky toes as *cambio de Dios*: God's spare change, God's afterthoughts.

If Wittgenstein were an animal, he would be either a dolphin or a chimpanzee. If Nietzsche were an animal, he'd be a velociraptor. If Heidegger were an animal, he'd be the same animal as Kant. Derrida would be a bird. Schopenhauer would be a bear. Freud would be a rooster. Deleuze would be a plant.

The book and my life are playing a nice game of catch lately.

Here lies Evan Lavender-Smith, a man who spent his life perfecting so many strategies of avoidance.

My wish for F.O.N. is that in its more serious moments it would provide great humor to an extraterrestrial race of beings, and in its humorous moments, great sadness.

How another thought will come along and *submerge* the one I was thinking.

The use of the word *academic* to mean conventional or a matter of course (e.g., *With a ten-stroke lead, this last putt for Tiger is purely* academic. . . .) reveals something about the world's perception of how I make my living.

The deliberate awkwardness of Wallace's prose is the affectation of a struggle with the limits of language.

"Dada, what noise?"

"Just my cell phone vibrating in my pocket, sweetie."

My tumultuous relationship with the semicolon.

Teaching is always a matter of closing my eyes and holding my breath.

A: I am simply *tormented* by my anxiety about death. I can hardly breathe! What should I do? What should I do?

B: (*handing A a Hershey's Chocolate Bar*) Perhaps you should eat more Hershey's Chocolate.

A: (*opening package, taking a bite*) Why, you're right! Hershey's Chocolate really does instantly dispel all thoughts of death! Thank you!

B: (*turning away from satisfied A*) Hershey's Chocolate, the solution to the riddle of life.

One way to read Heidegger is to replace the word *Being* with the word *TV*.

Seven people picketing outside the library, demanding that the IAU reinstate Pluto in the solar system.

How ridiculous to lament, "But I gave five years of my life to that cause!" As if one had something better to do.

The most prominent artificiality in any animated film is its adherence to the editorial and cinematographic conventions of live-action films.

"Al Qaeda is spoiling all our fun."

Desire for control is tenor to the vehicle which is my fear of death.

One finally *expects* meaning or truth to lie outside or beyond form; religion follows from the expectation of the possibility of transcendence. When Wittgenstein says, "*The solution to the riddle of life and death in space and time lies outside space and time,*" he is fully embracing this expectation, because Wittgenstein is transcendence crazy.

Selfish writing and selfless reading—and *vice versa*.

Nowadays, political conservatives cannot seem to produce art, so our designation of *conservatives* within the realm of "art" is, perforce, within the realm of so-called *political liberalism*—and it makes artists who consider themselves *politically liberal* very uncomfortable to be called *conservative* with respect to their "art," because the word connotes such a vile political persuasion. But that's exactly what it is, conservative "art." If you are a writer writing something called *stories*, you are most likely a right-wing "artist." Likewise if you are writing something called *poems* or *novels*, or if you are a filmmaker making something called *films*, or a painter making something called *paintings*.

Carmen: "*I Shaved My Balls for Nothing*, the new book by Evan Lavender-Smith."

The *truth* of any given entry is equal to zero. Combinations or accumulations of entries, however, may create a kind of *kinetic truth*.

"I have to break up with you because I'm beginning to feel that your *joi de vivre* is dulling my sense of the meaninglessness of life."

If there were a Viking Portable Lavender-Smith containing an abridgment of F.O.N., I would be very interested to read it, because there's no reason that the total value of the book couldn't be gained, through editorial happenstance, with much greater efficiency.

The "unknowability" of death. Qualifying death as "unknowable" is, finally, an act of cowardice; death as "unknowable" preserves mystery, the possibility of mystery. The true atheist knows death intimately; for him, there is nothing at all mysterious about death.

Perhaps they would be more palatable if *independent films* had more explosions in them.

"What are you up to this weekend?"

"Working on my screen adaptation of *Finnegans Wake.* You?"

"Same."

Generally, my favorite writer is the one I am currently reading.

Life is the point on which death pivots. Or: Death is the point on which life pivots.

The immanent and the transcendent are immanent to the book.

"Evan! You must choose between yourself and your son! One of you must die!"

"Easy—myself."

"Evan! You must now choose between your son and the notebook in your pocket!"

Long pause.

Homo sapiens, the miscarriage of evolution.

I would guess that approximately 50% of the time Carmen double-clicks on a filename, it results in her entering the Rename mode. *This is because she does not double-click quickly enough.* When my grandfather double-clicks on a filename he almost always—approximately 90% of the time—enters the Rename mode. This is because he panics when attempts to double-click and ends up *triple-* or *quadruple-*clicking.

"At a certain point one no longer felt estranged from one's contemporaries on account of space, but instead on account of time; at a later point one felt further estranged on account of virtual space; later, virtual time."

When I am sitting on the toilet in a public restroom and go to wipe, I place my book in the cubby provided by my underwear, down around my ankles.

On occasion, when distracted, I have forgotten the book and pulled up my underwear and pants with the book still inside. Even once, I buckled my belt and left the bathroom with the book in my underwear.

Some writers avoid writing about themselves at all costs. And we say to ourselves of such a writer, *He is thinking only about himself!*

There may be some question as to F.O.N.'s status as fiction, poetry, philosophy, nonfiction, etc., but hopefully there will be no question about its status as a book.

I should like to teach at a university where the bathrooms are stocked with two-ply toilet paper.

F.O.N. might be said to formulate a representation of the author under the spell of the book.

"Sit down in chair, Dada."

"That's okay, sweetie. I'm fine standing."

"Come on, Ev. Sit down in chair."

What I say to Carmen when she doesn't let me order a shit-load of CDs and books from Amazon when we're totally broke: "Will you just love me, just for once? Will you please just for once be my friend?"

The highest compliment a philosopher could receive from a reader of his book: "I used to feel that way, too."

Getting up the motivation to grade student essays is like trying to pass a piece of shit through the eye of a needle.

Why am I so averse to the idea of classifying F.O.N. as poetry? —Because poetry doesn't sell.

Jordan called today to emphasize that Shakespeare's monologues are not interior but spoken, characters talking aloud to themselves, and there's a rhetoric of private performance involved in the act of talking to oneself, etc.

I was reminded of something that had happened earlier in the day: I was alone, watching Tiger play at the Deutsche Bank Invitational, and at a certain point I thought, "Is this the 17th or the 18th hole?" and immediately thereafter, spoke aloud, "The 18th!" and immediately thereafter, thought, "Of course not the 18th. The 17th," and immediately thereafter, spoke aloud, "The 17th!" This is an example of one of a number of ways in which I think and talk to myself: in what I perceive to be the *affected* manner of a dialogue between silent speech and audible speech, but which may actually be a real conversation between two of my selves.

Should the reader of F.O.N. expect the meaning or truth of the book to lie with its author? Does the truth/meaning of the book lie outside the book? There is an illusion of transcendent meaning, perhaps, "a life behind the words." The book and the reader are at opposite ends of a circuit. To attempt to somehow jump off the circuit and find the author is ridiculous. There's no reason for the reader to put down the book, except to die, or go to the bathroom.

"But why in the world would I read *fiction*?" —That person cannot be argued with, for she is *in the right*.

Smoking my *per diem* in the early evening, watching the sunset, thinking about death.

I have two students who are quite talented writers, and it just so happens that both of them have already been to war. Several months ago these two were on a battlefield in Iraq watching guts spill out of other eighteen-year-olds; now they're here in my classroom intently listening to me go on and on about thesis statements. Not only are they my only good writers, they're the only ones who aren't nodding off while I talk. Perhaps they imagine me as a *terrorist* or an *insurgent* to help keep awake.

When we were kids Justin and I would spend hours contemplating death to arrive at statements such as *Death must be a kind of not-even-blackness.*

In my teens when I read about someone with an extremely high IQ I always hoped the article would at least briefly mention his/her religious or spiritual inclinations, so that I could say, *This person is a genius and he/she believes in X, so perhaps X is something I could believe in.* In my twenties, reading such an article, I would hope for the article not to mention such a person's inclinations, so to say, *Thankfully the article didn't mock me with what are sure to be this genius's smug spiritual inclinations.*

Aphorisms are not statements of truth but only *statements which happened at that moment to apply.* I should never think to purge any aphorism or entry in the revision of the book on account of its *not seeming true*.

We are at once the animals being dissected and the scientists performing the dissection.

It's easy to forget that the reader is implicated in the first sentence of *Moby-Dick*. Ishmael's generosity toward his audience is part of what makes the book so profoundly enjoyable to read.

From Old Notebooks: A Trying-Out.

I received a chambered nautilus for my 29th birthday. I have never before held an object in my hands which spoke so forcefully, LOOK AT ME, IDIOT.

"Perhaps it is not sleeping with one's students that is important, but only the knowledge that one could have had one attempted to." Brief meditative pause. "No, certainly it is *the experience of sleeping with them* that is most important."

I imagine myself waking up in the middle of the night to find an armed intruder raping Carmen or murdering Jackson and Sofia—but I am too tired to intervene.

Random line from Michael Bay's *The Rock*: "Greenlight the Seal incursion."

My children provide a very thin layer of insulation between death and me.

Practically every time lightning strikes nowadays, Carmen says, "It's an inconvenient truth."

From Old Notebooks: A Documentary Novel.

How excited I am about a thought after it has grown in my mind, after I have sufficiently nurtured it and prepared it for the world! But in the very moment I decide to let it out, I recognize some terrible, unforeseen error, but I can't stop myself now, it's too late. . . .

The problem of life and death seems complex only because we are scared.

Jackson in front of a mirror: "Hi, Jackson. Hi! How doing? Good! How doing, Jackson? Good, good. Okay! Bye-bye, Jackson. Okay, Jackson, bye-bye! See you in a couple days!"

Perhaps I insist on calling F.O.N. a novel because I'm leaving all the crap in.

I'm often moved to tears by a certain brand of violence in popular cinema from feeling so *ashamed*. An emotion I regularly experience with cinema, shame.

The creation of the concept of beauty originally requires the context of mortality.

How many cases of English Department paper I've gone through printing out drafts of short stories.

"The form of the book, the form of the posthumous collection of the famous writer's notebooks—is this an *appropriate* form, given that you are neither dead nor famous?"

"But in fact I am quite famous to myself. And I have been dead for an eternity, until very recently."

Is what I call *fear of death* the same thing as what a Christian would call *fear of eternal damnation*? —Contra non-being, eternal damnation seems to me like eternal paradise!

"Hey hon, wanna smoke some P-O-T and then F-U-C-K?"

"I don't necessarily have to live forever. A couple million more years will suffice."

When reading a contemporary *literary novel* or *book of poetry* one senses the author has gone through with a fine-toothed comb looking for anything that isn't smart.

It's important that a philosopher attempt to dismiss everything she's ever thought or said or written every time she thinks or says or writes. It's important for her to avoid at all costs building a *system of thought*.

Once the reader sits down in the theater of the book, I am free to get up and go to the bathroom.

There is no riddle to life for Sequoia not because she isn't smart—although she's definitely not; she's the dumbest dog

I've ever owned—but because the past and the future are irrelevant to her.

"One of the cardinal differences between man today and man 2000 years ago is that the latter did not possess MDMA."

Whether my preoccupation with death represents a limitation to and of my thinking or whether it is an extra-intelligent disposition, like preoccupation with sports. I can easily imagine the evolutionary psychologist's take on this.

Not a philosophy of presence—a present philosophy.

David Foster Wallace is at his very best when he transforms the temperature of a particular mode of language from cold to warm.

I am an ashamed American as well as a shameful American.

If there were a university that had a Department of Comedy and Philosophy—I meant to write Comedy and Tragedy—that is where I would most like to teach.

From Old Notebooks as a record of my son's linguistic development.

Certainty is always better located in the mind of a person other than oneself.

F.O.N. might tend toward a recognition of the impossibility of identity and subjectivity. —And then what?

They should sell beef jerky and Red Bull at the entrance, not the exit, to Home Depot.

"*Ryobi* must be Japanese for *shit*."

My apparent decision to put off *the hard work of spirituality* until some nebulous critical mass of books has been read.

It is, finally, *illogical* to say that what we say in one moment will be true, or even pertain, the next moment.
    So what do we do? We keep talking.

Ninety-five thousand American flags were passed out at last night's Vikings–Redskins game to celebrate the fifth anniversary of 9/11. When the Redskins scored a touchdown, people waved their flags like crazy.

The excitement-melancholy of Monday Night Football and the excitement-melancholy of terror are so similar because they have both been dimensionalized (hyperdimensionalized) by the liquid-crystal image. We respond to the immediacy of this dimensionalization, to the supraform of the image, rather than to the old notion of the pre-hyperdimensional form and content of the image, which no longer exist divorced from supraformal liquid-crystal dimensionalization. Our response to LCD, whether the pre-hyperdimensionalized form-content be Monday Night Football, or terror, or anything else, is the same *defeated* response: excitement-melancholy.

This is why I am able to say to Carmen, "I'm completely indifferent to what we choose to watch on TV this evening because I'll enjoy whatever we watch with equal and tremendous excitement-melancholy, so long as the volume is high."

If I sit silently in an empty room for a certain length of time something interesting is bound to happen.

"What the heck." "Holy shoot." "What the frick." "Darn it." "Son of a biscuit." "Shucks." "What the fudge." "Son of a gun."

Mark Z. Danielewski is blurring the distinction between novelist and video game designer.

Although the novel does not quite make it onto the book, the novel is still somewhere inside the book?

If I were to get a tattoo, it would be on the back of my hand, and it would read either FEED THE DOG or TAKE YOUR PILL.

"Show the terrorists what you're made of. Watch Monday Night Football."

When I attempt to *hypostatize* or *concretize* the abstractions pursuant to Heideggerian or Badiouvian ontology, I find myself resorting to, say, the *mere* universe, to *mere* cosmology.

This is very telling: The most acute sense of embarrassment I have felt in recent years occurred when I came upon two people at a party whom I thought I had just then overheard whispering something about me, and I asked them to reveal what it was they had been saying, and they playfully insisted that they were not talking about me, but I was sure that they had been so I persisted in my demand to know what it was they had been saying, and they continued to playfully insist

I was mistaken, and I continued to persist in my demand to know, and this exchange continued and continued until it became very uncomfortable, upon which time one of them emphatically declared, *We were not talking about you, Evan! Get over it!*

Philosophers can be as self-conscious as imaginable about knowledge or being, but they rarely seem to be very self-conscious about the presentation of this self-consciousness.

I hope to truly enjoy teaching one day, but it will have to be under the right circumstances. For example, at a university that doesn't frown upon its professors getting loaded before lecture.

When I *give voice* to a thought I am particularly proud of, I often add pauses and interjections such as *uh* and *sort of like* in order to make what I say sound unpremeditated.

The more students I teach, the more my students look like people I've known in my life. It's as if the classroom is a dream in which the students' faces have been abstracted from the faces of people I've known in my waking life.

A perception of beauty can *stabilize* the vertigo of philosophy.

My greatest wish is that in the moment after I die I feel like a man who has just leapt out from a corner to frighten a child but has found the child wearing an expression which asks, *What is it you were attempting to accomplish by leaping out at me like that?*

Even intelligent and passionate men will waste their lives watching sports—for the sense of implication.

The word *peradventure.*

Heidegger would have us believe that the whole of *Being and Time* was spoken in a single breath—i.e., outside of time—which is in stark contradiction to the theme of his book.

How many people at NMSU have noticed that a slightly different kind of toilet paper has been stocked in the bathrooms this semester?

    Sure, but how many people have *written* about it?

Someone might call F.O.N. a post-theoretical memoir.

It is no longer noble to say, *I disagree with this or that American policy, but I still remain, at heart, a proud American.* Nowadays the only noble thing to say with respect to being an American is, *I am deeply ashamed to be an American, and I wish to disassociate myself with America.*

It befits Gogol to be the greatest writer whose existence one regularly forgets.

Contemporary American literature is a kind of performance art that takes place at writer's conferences.

Today Sofia's last remaining congenital pimple—whitehead near right nostril—disappeared.

I am always astounded to learn that Barthes's *tmesis* is a regular practice for readers. Am I deceiving myself when I say that I read every word of what I read?

    The fastest pace at which I read in my head is equivalent to the fastest pace at which I could read the same words in my mouth. The possibility of reading in my head at a pace faster than this sends me hurtling into the brick-wall boundary of my intelligence.

It does seem odd that I haven't yet taught an English class in NMSU's Poultry Building.

My desire to get a Ph.D. coincides with my desire not to have to do any real work in my life.

It can be a terrible feeling to suddenly remember that the sun is a star.

From Old Notebooks: A Reality Novel.

If I had to bet on the physical scenario of my own death, I would bet heart attack on the toilet.

But for the smell, it could be great fun to go back to Berkeley for a Ph.D.

One suspects that the contemporary poet and book reviewer have something in common: they both keep a grab bag of certain words next to the keyboard.

When I was young I would look up at the sky and ask God for a sign of his existence: no sign would come, so I would focus my attention on a pile of bricks, and nothing would happen, the pile of bricks would remain exactly the same, so I would wait and wait and continue to focus and continue to focus, I would point all of my faith in the direction of the bricks, *I would attempt to knock the pile of bricks over with my soul*, but nothing would happen and still nothing would happen, and so finally, after a long while of this, I would turn my attention toward something else, something more likely to move, a shrub, and I would concentrate on the shrub with all my might, I would direct *every last ounce of my faith in the beneficence and omnipotence of God toward the shrub*, but nothing would happen, and nothing would continue to happen, so finally I would give God one last chance to prove his existence to me, *or else . . .* and then the wind would blow and the shrub would move.

And I would receive the gift of the miracle of the shrub's movement graciously and humbly and go about the rest of my day with reinvigorated certain knowledge of God's existence.

If a thought must be let out, it would best be directed toward the nether region between poetry and prose.

"The Influence of Jack Handy on Lavender-Smith's *From Old Notebooks*."

"Dada, I need help."
   "So do I, sweetie. So do I."

A man exiting his car to help another man push his stalled car to safety.
   We are each terribly alone in the world.

For the past few days I have each day witnessed what I perceived to be a nebulous black form moving across proximate space in my peripheral vision. And it has only just now occurred to me that there is a type of mind—and this type may very well represent the majority of them, at least in the U.S.— that would immediately conclude this black form to be *of the supernatural*. I may have concluded the same as a child, and I may have become momentarily terrified, physically terrified, the same sensation I often feel supremely nostalgic for and now only feel when watching a horror film.
   Perhaps one way to get through life is to watch a great number of horror films. It could only be a matter of scaring

oneself into such a state that questions of life and death recede. To live in a state of constant physico-mental fear, to live constantly in the *horripilant state*.

The structure of the book might best be represented thus:

. . . the book, the book, the book, the book, the book . . .

The combination of Spike Lee and Terrance Blanchard often results in a melancholy patriotism.

How rather than with a teddy bear Jackson prefers to sleep cuddled up with a couple of pieces of trash from the bathroom wastebasket. He'll sleep cuddled up with a cardboard toilet paper roll, an empty tube of toothpaste.

If I were accepted to a Ph.D. program somewhere, I would have to make it very clear to the Department Chair or whomever that I couldn't possibly be expected to *interact with other students*. Furthermore, I would need to be assured that under no condition would I ever be expected to *take any classes*, let alone write some sort of *essay* or *dissertation*. And it must never be that I am put in the degrading position of having to receive a *grade* on something.

Even the slightest trace of mechanical reproduction—a cap from a bottled water—acts as counterforce to my death anxiety.

Sometimes when I write *the book* I seem to mean something in between *this book* and *a book*.

The lower the tone at which the piss hits the water, the longer the penis?

To suggest that the possibility of infinite play within a finite structure is redemptive is tantamount to suggesting *Enjoy Coke!* is redemptive—which, I have no doubt, it can be.

It has come to that unfortunate pass at which we must now require all poets to enroll in a standardized credentialing program. If they do not gain and maintain the proper credentials, they will be prosecuted for their poetry.

This may seem dangerous, but surely not as dangerous as millions of bad poems.

The parody of sincerity has become the new real sincerity: We feel that certain moments in *Austin Powers* and *Happy Gilmore* are emotional moments because the films have one-upped sincere or vulgar sincerity with parody, and yet have still remained sincere.

When I was young, I couldn't simply use the computer and be happy about it, I had to take the computer apart, piece by piece, until I had destroyed it. So it is with me and *everything*.

It would now seem that our universe may have originated at the hand of beings not very unlike ourselves.

When I imagine myself dying before the completion of F.O.N., I imagine Carmen or Mc transcribing the remaining handwritten entries from my notebooks and adding them to the end of the typed text word for word; I see and hear myself shouting from atop a giant iceberg, "Idiots! I had them completely fooled until now!"

Cinema is the retarded younger sibling of the novel.

Living in New York, one might encounter many *wiggers*. Living in New Mexico, one encounters many *wavajos*.

Another difference between F.O.N. and philosophy is that every work of philosophy I've read purports to have a context beyond the book.

Over the past five years I've spent approximately $10,000 on cell phone bills, yet there is nothing I hate more than talking on the phone.

Professor A: "It is an unspoken truth in the department that philosophy is *over*, and that we might as well all be *history professors* now."

Professor B: "Let's just hope the provost doesn't find out."

The more domestic tragedies the United States suffers (9/11, Hurricane Katrina, etc.), the greater the opportunity for the anniversary of tragedy to coincide with Monday Night Football, the greater the potential poignancy of Monday Night Football.

Monday Night Football mobilizes this country to feel.

Death has very white teeth.

The greatness of a certain type of poet—a poet like Stein, for example—may be determined by her ability to let go of her control over language in a very controlled manner.

From Old Notebooks: A Pity Party.

The ESPN MNF commentators are adept at alternating between clichéd humanistic quips and insightful football quips. (Except for Joe Theismann, who doesn't seem to care to play this game, who wants only to concentrate on *football*, which, as we now know, is the *least interesting part of Monday Night Football*. For Theismann's unwillingness to pretend to care about the world-beyond-football we hope he'll not be back next season.)

One marvels that the human race has survived so long given the indomitable vexation which is the human-toddler temper tantrum.

The book has nothing to do with the author's life, but only with the author's life in the book, that is to say, with the reader's life.

The word *autohagiography*.

I certainly didn't expect to cry during two of this season's first three telecasts of Monday Night Football.

I am always in a foreign country with philosophy.

I feel like I should save the bottle once I've finished it, as a sort of battle trophy.

The car jolting to a stop at an intersection; Jackson jostled in his car seat, yelling at me disapprovingly: "Be *careful*, Dada. My *Jackson*. Okay, Dada? Be *careful*. My *Jackson*."

The ideal postmodern reader (the computer) could conceivably perform an operation of *reverse engineering* on a text by which *sites of revision* are uncovered and from them, *rough drafts*.

How wonderful if F.O.D. really did turn out to be my symptom.

The nightmare of technology coming alive and overtaking human civilization is finally realized when my cell phone vibrates and inches across the table.

The poet and philosopher should abandon themselves of the categories poetry and philosophy and their writing should consist of this abandonment.

From Old Notebooks as, finally, an attempt to reprioritize my writing in relation to my family.

The tyranny of the image over memory. When they do the death montage at the Oscars I always find myself thinking, *I'd forgotten he died, I'd forgotten she died, I'd completely forgotten he died.* . . . Likewise, I'll intently watch every game of the World Series and a month later be unable to say what teams played.

Here's a ridiculous thought: In imagining the instant of my death, I always ward off death for a moment longer so I can take one last breath—*because I deserve it.*

No matter what I'm reading now, I misread it in order to make it apply to F.O.N.

The distinction between philosopher and scholar is analogous to that between poet and critic. University philosophy departments rarely contain philosophers, just as English departments rarely contain poets. When I *take a position* in a department, I plan to *hang my art on the hat rack* at the entrance to the building.

The ideal teaching position at a university would be one in which I don't actually have to teach a class, but could simply hang around the department a few times a week and meet people. Better yet, sit in my office with the door *closed and locked.*

Treating my children as objects of study rather than children. *The phenomenon of my family.*

From Old Notebooks: An Affair with Philosophy.

The art on the walls inside Pizza Hut is actually enlarged clip art.

The impossibility of knowing is where all avenues of knowledge finally lead.

Carmen referred to us as *soul mates* today when I was struggling to find language to describe the same. Hers is the correct term, and I would have continued searching in vain: I have always associated *soul mates* with watermelon bubblegum, magnetic earrings, and the question, *Do you swear to God?*

Even in my wildest dreams is life the most tragic condition imaginable.

Even in a book like *Zarathustra* or *Either/Or*, the intent of the author is omnipresent, if only because he's working to hide it; we still see the author's hand extend from the page of the book to feed us some truth food.

What we are searching for is a practice whereby philosophy may or may not be subsequent to the production of a book: 1) We make a book. 2) If philosophy happens, we're happy for it.

Whenever I first begin talking aloud to myself it is as if I am singing along with my thoughts.

It has become a cliché to say that there is a time and place for cliché.

F.O.N. might best be termed a *documentary*. I am aware of the book in much the same way as the subject of the documentary is, in cinema, the camera.

I often have the sensation that my body will fail me without a moment's notice, that one moment I will be the paragon of health and vigor and the next I'll be struggling to take my one last romantic breath. I feel like the success or failure of my organs is up for grabs, I imagine my heart as a sort of lazy asshole in my chest.

Ours is a liberalism of compromise. We have no Left left.

It's extraordinary how long it has taken the *linguistic turn* in philosophy to trickle down into the form of the philosophy. So far language has been no more than one of philosophy's many *concerns*.

There is a type of writing, of which Kafka may be master, in which the political referent forever slips from the grasp of allegory. *Kafkaesque* may refer first of all to the trace of the political.

When the planes struck the WTC, and struck again and again and again and again, we knew there was a "philosophical problem" at hand, simulacrum something, but we couldn't quite wrap our minds around it because the force of the image wouldn't allow for it—but that itself was the problem. We felt as if the planes had struck our cerebral cortexes, our epistemes, when all they really struck were some buildings on TV.

"Dada, those fish dead."

"No they're not, sweetie. Look, they're swimming around."

"Yes, Dada. Look. Fish dead."

"No they're not. They're alive. They're swimming around. Fish alive. Look."

"Fish dead, Dada."

"You don't even know what that word means. Stop saying it. That's a no-no word. Fish alive, fish alive."

"Fish dead."

"Okay, if you say that word one more time you're getting a time-out."

Looking at the pictures of the literature and philosophy professors on websites at universities, I can tell by his or her face what sort of a prose each professor writes, and none of it is very interesting.

"Does everybody read in their head with a British accent or is it just me?"

I know that the reconciliation of my writing life and my family life is one of the things F.O.N. is finally *about*, but I can't actually *see it* in the book; I don't imagine I could point to an entry and say, *Here is an example of that*. (I could perhaps point to the *entire book*—or the bags under my eyes.) There may not be textual evidence to demonstrate this, but the vacillation of my life's two halves from a state of harmony to a state of discord represents the *sine qua non* of the book's existence.

Is it a coincidence that Frank Gehry's teeth and hair look so much like his buildings?

From Old Notebooks: A Joke Book.

Aphorisms are selfish statements wearing the clothes of selfless statements.

Instead of think tanks to address problems of foreign policy, think tanks to address the problem of death.

No matter how many times they're washed our sheets and pillowcases still smell like Jackson vomit.

I often read in a state of frenzied panic, as one will read who is placed in a sealed room with a limited supply of oxygen and told that among the big stack of books in the corner is a single sentence which holds the key to the creation of oxygen from paper.

I have more than once entertained a reverie in which I imagine the primary audience for my writing to be a panel of extraterrestrial beings.

Wittgenstein's poetry peeks out at us from behind the not-poetry—the philosophy?

Wittgenstein's is a parenthetical poetry.

The plot of the book has been displaced by the action of a mind.

In their later work, Ligeti and Gehry and Markson are not postmodernists *per se*, although much of their work *seems* postmodern. It might be said that the body of their work is postmodernist, while the spirit of their work is modernist. They have learned from postmodernism; it's as if they are modernists who appropriate form and style, as they find it useful, from postmodernism.

Too long steeping the riddle of life, time to drink it down.

In my writing I sometimes feel the need to overexplain certain everyday things, like the function of a fork or the phenomenon of atmospheric precipitation, as if my audience died thousands of years ago or will be born thousands of years hence.

Mom used to say that if anyone should have been born into the aristocracy, it should have been me. I'm not exactly sure why she said that, but I strongly agree.

It may be that in future years I will look back on my life as divided into two parts: 1) Those years during which I rarely wore shorts or flip-flops. 2) Those years during which I was a husband and father.

The book is the subject and the object of the book.

A feature of Wittgenstein's philosophical aesthetic: He increases the pace of the writing in order to direct us to *feel* a false assumption. This is why he loves lists.

The word *nincompoop*.

In the bathroom at Albertsons today it occurred to me that I had thought about death in this bathroom before.

I was once told by a gay man that a widower will wear the clothes of his recently deceased spouse as part of his grieving process, and I mistakenly understood him to mean a man wearing a woman's clothes, but I now know he meant a man wearing another man's clothes. The image of a grieving man wearing his recently deceased wife's red polka-dotted dress yet remains among the most heartbreaking images of my life.

The single thing I have most loved in watching Jackson grow has been keeping up with the minutiae of his language acquisition, watching as he becomes human one word at a time.

Consciousness is my worst habit.

When we read philosophy, we sit on the edge of our seat waiting for the philosopher to say something we can really use, to say something really *definitive*, but as soon as he does, we scoff, slam the book closed. *If he says it with such definitiveness, then surely it can't be true!*

We feel lucky we weren't in the buildings when they col-lapsed, specifically, that we didn't *stay* in the buildings after they had been struck—although we were in Iowa or Florida or New Mexico at the time.

From Old Notebooks might end like this:
   Las Cruces
   2006
   or like this:
   Des Moines–Philadelphia–Des Moines–Pennsauken–Las Cruces–Berkeley–Las Cruces
   1977–2006.

Perhaps I am not enjoying having children to the degree I would had I had children in my mid- or late thirties, because now, at 29, my soul is still raging over the loss of its youth.

   I suspect it should be done raging in a few years, however.

There's little in nature I like as much as lightning. I like it for many reasons, not the least of which is that it is a quick re-minder of my complete alienation from the world.

Joy, rather than *error*, is the better antonym to *truth*.

Story entitled "Futureless" about a nostalgic 29-year-old part-time instructor at a community college who begins shooting heroin with one of his 17-year-old students after class.

Culture is the food of philosophy. In the age of the internet, the excrement of a Parisian philosopher and the excrement of a New Mexican philosopher should smell a lot alike.

Jackson: "How doing, Baby Sista, how doing?"
 "Gaaaaaaah . . . gaaaaaaah."
 "Good, good. How's work going?"

It is true that F.O.N. is written by at least as many authors as it has entries—and none of them is me. This is why I will never be able to speak for the book. Because the *I* who would speak for it is not among those who wrote it.

How Carmen refers to what she uses to style her hair as, simply, *product*.

It is in keeping with the spirit of postmodernism to use terms like *high postmodernism* or *late postmodernism* to describe works that are barely five minutes old.

Writing is my religion is a ridiculous thing to say, but it is nevertheless true that there is a mystery known to the believer through faith which shares something with that known to the writer through writing. Likewise the child its toy, the dog its bone.

What formal feature of the book am I forgetting to address? How am I still hiding behind the book?

Have I thought to include the simple statement that I am very, very afraid—*of absolutely everything*? But surely that's obvious enough.

The barber paradox. I have a student who happens to be my barber. I have not received a haircut since the semester began because I would not feel at all comfortable having my hair cut by my student, on the one hand, and, on the other hand, I would not feel at all comfortable coming to class to reveal to my student that I had received a haircut by some other, imposter barber. So I have had to content myself with my hair looking like shit, on the one hand, and on the other, the obvious disillusionment—always glancing sidelong at my awful hair—of my barber.

Jeremy James Lavender-Smith, b. 6 October 1976, d. 6 October 1976.

Carmen's use of the word *scandalous.*

The only way I know how to write is monomaniacally.

When I read an academic essay with a bunch of block quotes strewn throughout, I know I'm bound to hate it, because 99% of the time the professor or Ph.D. candidate who wrote it is using block quotes as filler, just like we used to do in middle school.

It is understood in academia that in order for a humanities professor to get tenure, he has to publish papers, and to publish papers, sustain an argument for a certain duration, and to sustain an argument for a certain duration, rely on irrelevant block quotes.

How embarrassing for the whole of academia that block quotes, of all things, represent your darkest secret!

Any person who has looked the inevitability of the void squarely in the face feels he is the only person to have ever done so. Surely that's part of the seduction to keep looking.

When I was a kid I sometimes felt *icky* about Shel Silverstein, as if there were *boundary issues* between us.

I suppose I'm asking the reader to treat me like a text, bully me around a bit.

Many of us who were once in love with it have become *mad at cinema*, and find that the healthiest thing to do is break up with it.

Perhaps one way the book could end would be by becoming a book entirely about the book, causing it to disappear underneath its own reflection.

Nightly Jackson wages war against sleep.

The old assertion that *meta-authorial forces write the text* has become difficult to apply to artistic works, as opposed to commercial works, because the artist applies the same interpretive apparatus from her end, which makes for schizoid reading: if such unintended meanings are felt to exist in an artistic work they are not so easily attributed to meta-authorial forces but instead to the cynical ambiguity of the text.

At best, art and religion offer simulations of redemption.

Short story which is a reformulation of "Rip Van Winkle" highlighting the great sadness felt by protagonist over having lost so much precious time.

When I imagine the final moment of my life, I imagine myself crying and the rest of the world laughing. A worthwhile goal is to become comfortable with the prospect of laughing along with the world in the final moment of one's life.

"Dada, why does time fly?"

One of the few vivid memories I have of my childhood is eating a bowl of peanuts and raisins every week while watching *Miami Vice*. I have no real memory of the show other than that it was turned on, but I can see the bowl of peanuts and raisins as if it were before me now.

In thinking about the *end* of F.O.N.—in every meaning of that word—I imagine myself on the nothing side of a world willing myself to push through to the something side.

Short story about a novelist on the operating table for open-heart surgery performed by a doctor who has read all his books.

It would have been ideal if Fredric Jameson were the one to provide the DVD commentary for Pixar's *Cars*.

I will happily write academic essays if someone places a gun to my head.

The gulf that separates a recognition of one's immortality from a recognition of one's mortality is the gulf of youth. The gulf that separates a recognition of one's mortality from a second recognition of one's immortality is the gulf of adulthood. The gulf of death could care less.

Wild animals I've seen in my neighborhood in past years: coyote, wolf, fox, rattlesnake, scorpion, tarantula, bobcat, rabbit, roadrunner, quail, horny toad, lizard, eagle, hawk, whooping crane, centipede, millipede, prairie dog, mouse, rat, skunk, and frog.

How ridiculous I must look, sitting at this table in a crowded library, again closing my eyes for fifteen seconds before jumping out of my chair to reach for my notebook and pen! A total freak!

My anxiety about ending the book mirrors my anxiety about death. Attempting to imagine the last entry is like attempting to imagine the instant of my death.

Death can't get me while I'm watching football.

When I imagine giving a reading from F.O.N., it is always a matter of imagining myself trying to make the best out of all the wrong tools.

Jackson calls lightning "*light-mmm-mmm.*"

We are startled to learn of a dream of science that has not yet been realized.

Short story entitled "The War on Weather": A few weeks after another global warming–induced natural disaster strikes the U.S., the president's press secretary comes on TV to announce that "the disarmament of the troposphere has begun."

"What are you up to this weekend?"
    "Just ballasting my philosophical edifice. You?"
    "Same."

Late postmodernism attempts to view the relationship between modernism and postmodernism dialectically.

The world keeps insisting that F.O.D. is aberrational. —But surely it can't be! Surely it is perfectly *status quo*!

I have roughly the same face in my mind for James Joyce, M.C. Escher, Sigmund Freud, and Sherlock Holmes.

Liberation from the tyranny of conceptual transcendence is perhaps too historically preordained, too historicityish, too successional: *All philosophers before me have insisted on X, so naturally I will insist on X_2. . . .*

The only thing that has improved my life more than discovering philosophy is discovering Prilosec.

Will I ever fully commit myself to total vulgarity, i.e., commit myself to writing the "big novel"?

Jackson's mastery of language, at nearly three years old, proceeds in a number of very different ways, among which is the process whereby he memorizes a string of words and parrots it for days or weeks until he happens to retrieve a component from the string, a single word, and the fact of the string's composition is finally revealed to him. We know what this is like: when, for example, a string of words serving as the title to a film that has always existed in our mind in a purely titular capacity (e.g., *Terms of Endearment*) suddenly functions grammatically (*terms of endearment*). The mistaking of parts and whole in order to arrive at an apprehension of both—that may be a formula for revelation.

Billions of years later/ the dead man's consciousness/ flickered awake/ in an empty expanse of space/ then back off.

One way to end the book would be to start repeating myself, *to forget the book*.

"Jackson, I have a trivia question for you. What's the name of Mama's brother?"

"I don't know."

"Think."

"I don't know."

"Think. . . ."

"My no think, Dada. My no like to think."

I should be honest with myself and admit that I talk shit about Wallace because I care about his writing very deeply.

"Narrative arc," "well-rounded characters," "suspension of disbelief" ... *all members of a statist narratology!*

When the supremely egocentric person is caught in a supremely egocentric act, his immediate course of defense is to proclaim that the person who caught him is behaving in a supremely egocentric manner.

I perceive a continuum between the immediate physical difficulty with which Mom attempts to relate to Jackson at the age of nearly three years and the distant physical difficulty with which she must have attempted to relate to me at that age.

I have become worried about the moon recently, as if something terrible were about to befall it.

Must the artifice of the book be increased in order for the book to end?

To gain a position by which I might comfortably stand in proximity to life instead of death.

One philosopher does some work, dies, and passes the baton to the next philosopher, who does some work, dies, passes the baton to the next, who works, dies, passes, etc. And in this way philosophy proceeds through time, along an oval course.

"At every moment life suffers the light of innumerable surrounding stars."

Not writing my way out of death, writing death out of my way.

In a universe of infinite time, we experience an infinite number of afterlives. In a universe of finite time, we experience none.

F.O.N. might contain a number of false endings.

If it's yellow, let it mellow. If it's brown, flush it down. If it's red—yikes—for the love of God, Carmen, flush it twice.

Short story about a husband and father of two who, exhausted near delirium after tiling his house's bathrooms, kitchen, dining room and hallway, tiles his house's walls and ceilings, then tiles his sleeping wife and children.

1) Think always about sex. 2) Have a family. 3) Think always about death.

Does the possibility of an apocalyptic death—for example, mass death following the explosion of the sun—ease the difficulty of death? If we were all to die together? Somehow, yes.

Short story about a tribe the members of which are not or pretend not to be aware of something we suppose they must be aware of (e.g., the existence of their hands and feet). Members of the tribe persist in pretending/not-knowing even when subjected to the most hideous forms of physical torture.

What would be truly remarkable in philosophy would be if a kid who grew up on PlayStation and Cocoa Puffs *rediscovered* the cogito.

By virtue of the process of accumulation, not the what-is-accumulated, does the book become greater than the sum of its parts.

One must always bear in mind it is sheer coincidence that *god* and *dog* are anagrams.

Story which describes a steel-cage death match between poetry, drama, fiction, nonfiction, and philosophy.

Most all recent thought privileges the new, the next. And by continuing to privilege the new, we already doom our contemporary new, our precious newly new, to immediate antiquation. Deleuze was very new—but only for a moment—now he's very old, as old as Descartes.

How do we build *alongside* Deleuze and Descartes, instead of *upon* them? We formalize—give artistic form to—our philosophy.

The genre of the book—poetry, fiction, nonfiction, philosophy—might largely depend on the reader's mood.

Novella in which adult protagonist does not possess knowledge of the fact of death.

Disposing of the cigarette in the car's ashtray rather than tossing it out the window: saving the planet one cigarette butt at a time.

The book is not a machine but a point of rendezvous for many machines.

Story about protagonist who harbors secret dread of life and death, and who, late in life, meets someone who harbors same dread. Protagonist befriends the latter and for the first time in his life is not consumed by dread.

Five-hundred-year floods every other year now.

"No way documennary. My watch Nemo, Dada."

Rocking Sofia to sleep in my arms, I imagine a beer bottle shattering against her forehead. I *shake the thought off* like a man who prowls the city at night so often squinting his eyes and smacking the side of his head with his hand to rid his mind of *sick fantasy*. My thoughts have a will that is not my will, or a will that I refuse to acknowledge as my own.

My thoughts *jut away* from me—I *yank* them back.

I sometimes worry that I will not understand the future: those things that are the most obvious and simplest to other people will be incomprehensibly complex to me. I often romanticize my imagined obsolescence.

Have I said this already?

Novella about a world-famous author who sustains a severe head injury debilitating his literary genius. Proceeds to revise all of his earlier works for the worse.

The violation we feel when Jackson eagerly watches a television commercial targeted at his age group.

From Old Notebooks: A Documentary. From Old Notebooks: A Documentary Book. From Old Notebooks: A Thought Documentary.

The *interpretive dominant* of outsider art would be the locating of the work in relation to the tyranny of culture, just as the interpretive dominant of extraterrestrial art would be the locating of the work in relation to the tyranny of life.

Dad: "I don't get lonely."

The $x_1 \ldots x_2 \ldots x_3 \ldots$ character of philosophy, the *successional* or *technological* character of philosophy, is what one might best refer to as the *machismo of philosophy*.

The rhythm of the book accords with the rhythm of a life.

Having children does not aid in one's quest for salvation—having children merely ups the stakes.

Having children makes the impossibility of salvation that much more intolerable.

After attempting to demonstrate to my students how someone might arrive at an abstract thought, a student came to my desk and said, *It's all, like, so emotional, what you said about my thoughts.* . . . The rewards of meta-intellection are meta-intellectual.

The outlandish suggestion that the entire history of a language is contained in any contemporary utterance of the language might be likened to the scientific fallacy of Cuvier's synecdochic bone. But with the discovery of DNA Cuvier was, in a sense, proved correct. It would not surprise me to learn that linguists of the distant future could extrapolate the entire development of an ancient language if they possessed from it only a single television commercial.

Upon learning that the sound in a seashell is not the sound of the ocean, young protagonist's childhood ends.

"I may say some things that will shock and terrify you, things that will seem to suggest the world has no meaning, but I've always got some *spare meaning up my sleeve*." Spare-meaning-up-the-sleeve is the gift of philosophy, given to us by the Santa Clauses of philosophy.

My favorite muse is disillusionment.

It may be *organic* for the self-reflexivity to *grow* over the course of the book, but I'm becoming so very eager for it to *die*.

Character who discovers that his depression of past years can be attributed to the color of the tinting on his sunglasses.

"Dada, why those plants dead?"
    "I don't know, sweetie."
    "Why those plants dead, Dada?"
    "Because . . . I don't know why, sweetie."
    "Dada, those plants dead because . . . that's the deal?"

It seems odd that I have not been to a museum of olfactory art, or ever heard of such a thing.

Doing philosophy is performing thought performing. Philosophy is always a performance of a performance, meta-performance. What we need in order reduce these dimensions of performance by one—the most we can hope for—is an aesthetics of philosophy.

Character who all his life mistook the word *race* in *human race* for a verb.

The relationship between the events of my life, the events of the book, and the events of someone's reading of the book is not a relationship of substantive correspondence, but of modal correspondence. When I imagine the relationship of one set of events to another set as like the curves at either end of a carpenter's scribe, the tip is always breaking off the pencil side, or is always being lifted and placed back down so that the curve it draws is irregularly broken to the curve at the scribe's other end, which is, perhaps, also irregularly broken.

The word *bugbear*. Death is my *bugbear*.

Novel with every tenth line numbered in the margin.

While my instinct may be to open the door for everyone, I especially tend to open the door *for women*, which is, finally, a means by which I attempt to dominate women. By holding the door open for a woman, am I not saying to her, "You must pass by me in order to proceed," as well as, "and you'd better be grateful for it"?

Art installation entitled *Posthumous Masturbation*.

"I'm so out of shape I get winded trying to drink my Frappuccino through a straw."

The difference between *thinking to myself* and *talking to myself*—when there is a difference, first, and when the difference is not solely a matter of a difference between things like *images* and *words*, second—is a difference I might spend my whole life trying to comprehend.

Reading over the transcription of F.O.N., I feel alienated from the reflection of myself therein: Is this me? Was this ever me? Is this the biggest put-on of my life? Have I only been *performing myself* this whole time? But it must have felt right *then*, just as it does *now*.

Justin's dad reminding me of Sean Connery is simply a matter of a similar sparkle in their eyes; Carmen's brother's eyes and Jackson's share the same sparkle, which is why those two look so much alike.

    Bedroom eyes, a woman called Jackson's eyes.

Short story anthology of stories left unfinished at death of authors.

I seem to be assuming, in writing this book, there are people in the world who might actually care about what I think.

From Old Notebooks: A Sonata.

Scene in which an author, who happens to be carrying one of his books as he walks, is shot at on the street. Author attempts to block bullets with book.

"I love you one."

    "I love you too, Dada."

Our response to Deleuze is, "And death? Where is death? Has he forgotten death?" Our response to Cioran is, "Grow up! Stop thinking so much about death!"

A person who, exteriorly unprovoked, laughs aloud—he is my brother.

I am saddened and terrified by the prospect of introducing Jackson and Sofia to *a world of adults* in which images of violent death are bandied about so irresponsibly, in which they are so commonly and carelessly exploited as the ideal vehicle for emotional manipulation.

Play entitled *The One Is Not* for which only one real ticket is sold to The One. Prior to performance, life of The One is clandestinely researched by spies of theater and a dossier is provided to playwright who intersperses references particular to the life of The One throughout an otherwise conventional play. As references reach a certain pitch, other audience members of the theater (all actors) slowly turn heads toward The One, who is seated somewhere near the middle of the theater, and the play dwindles as actors on stage one by one turn to stare directly at The One. Theater lights come up. Silence.

We feel confident there will be no Super Bowl XMV. But what about Super Bowl CCV?

Cinema as a vehicle for thought or philosophy, as in Deleuze, affords cinema the illusion of being *useful* just as it would were the occasion of taking a date to the cinema to result in getting laid that night.

Short play: A replica of *Guernica* is carted in from offstage to center stage by ARTIST whose clothes bear fresh paint splatters. Small hole already burning outward from painting's center. Camcorders and lights arranged across stage, aimed toward painting. ARTIST races across stage to climb ladder and stand on platform in loft waiting for hole in painting to enlarge. ARTIST grasps trapeze bar, jumps off platform, flies across stage, releases bar just before reaching painting, flies through painting knocking over painting and cart, camcorders and lights. ARTIST lies unmoving among debris, painting continues to burn.

    CURTAIN catches fire.

By placing quotation marks around certain entries I am creating some sort of hierarchy of bullshit.

I attempt to revise against my will, in a direction perpendicular to my will. I attempt to destroy my will in the work wherever I find it.

To get my nearly illiterate community college students to really *feel* that all of philosophy is at stake every time they sit down to have a conversation about it.

A man riding with another man on a motorcycle must choose between safety—holding on to the man in front of him—and the appearance of possible homosexuality. American men will risk their lives so as to not appear possibly gay.

Dreaming more and more about bad weather and old friends.

How do I end the book when my life is suddenly contained by the book?

A good goal for old age is never to second-guess oneself about inviting one's grandchildren over for dinner.

I enjoy TV so much because it rarely tries very hard to be art.

I am in a *showdown* with the person in the adjacent stall to see who will break the silence and fart first.

From Old Notebooks: A Work-in-Progress.

"May I can please have some grape juice, Dad?"

Short story the narrative occasion of which is the mutation of the language gene in humans 200,000 years ago.

They should offer an M.F.A. in philosophy.

The readily accessible faith nowadays is faith in the machine: the computer, the body, the brain.

What trace of transcription remains of F.O.N.'s conversion from notebook to word processor?

Story in which young author digs a very long and narrow ditch in desert, places long piece of dental floss in ditch. Fills ditch up with dirt, pats smooth. His "first novel."

I imagine that a unique feature of F.O.N. is that were one to read it backwards it would be no better or worse than reading it forwards, but only different. (Perhaps sadder?)

Short story about twin brothers surgically removed from mother's womb and placed in identical rooms equipped with surveillance cameras. Parents sit in surveillance room observing television monitors, ordering entry of stimuli into rooms, carefully noting differences in brothers' physical responses.

Play: A very large stage occupied by fifteen actors in groups of three, each group engaged in isolated action/dialogue. The audience's attention will be split five ways. As in Ligeti, the action of one component will occasionally meet up with and join the action of another, then part.

Sequoia walks into a bar and orders a Sofia vomit on the rocks.

Contemporary American philosophy—it even sounds wrong.

I feel like a jerk when I use *her* as my indefinite singular possessive pronoun, an even bigger jerk when I use *his*, and a deaf-mute when I use *his/her*.

That nihilism follows from considered joy—that is the tragedy of thought.

Short story which imagines a series of viable *foetus in foetus*, nested fetuses. Ten generations born in a matter of hours.

How scared I once was of reading philosophy.
    How scared I still am.

"I love you, Dada. Don't go anywhere without me."

Short short story about an eight-year-old Samuel Beckett climbing up then deliberately falling from a tall tree. Branches break his fall. Climbs back up, falls, climbs back up, falls. Repeats, repeats.

The book perhaps contains as many beginnings as it has entries, but not so many endings.

Poem about a late-blooming poet.

Film which concerns, in its entirety, protagonist's flight from the camera.

"We're each entitled to our own opinion—except for you."

Character in story eats page after page.

I hardly notice Sequoia until Carmen and the kids are out of town, but once they're gone I expect her to go back to being my very best friend, as it was between us before I met Carmen.

That is so typical of me with friends.

Play in which all dialogue is paraphrased in stage directions.

Story about a boy who continues to refer to himself only in the third person all through childhood and into adulthood.

"A Narratological Approach to Deleuze and Guattari's *A Thousand Plateaux*."

"Let's pretend to be on Ecstasy and have a really great talk."

Novel which is simply a list of answers to every conceivable question that could be asked of it.

Philosophy has forgotten the book.
   —Did it ever know it?

Short story about a character who suffers from the condition of double touch.

Where doubt ends, and what happens after doubt, that is when we call foul. But the true skeptic would have called foul long before doubt.

"Dada's got you."

We can't entirely give up our belief that the world is ours alone.

Perhaps the status of the book as a novel is finally a matter of faith.

Short story about a world in which all points of destination are connected by a bridge.

A philosophical system the foundational statement of which is not the cogito but rather an unintelligible grunt.

Short story about an artist composing thirty or more major works simultaneously.

How much shame will I one day feel about F.O.N?

Story entitled "The Accidental Plagiarist."

I would be interested to see the results of a survey concerning the religious tendencies of middle-aged people without children.

Essay entitled "Genre Trouble."

"All this talk of global warming is killing my buzz."

Essay entitled "Swinging for the Bleachers, or, How to Write a *Tour de Force*."

We feel it is our duty to study life, because who else is going to?

Short story about a character who must use speech to think.

Badiou would probably call F.O.N. a *disaster*.

There is a certain type of author who uses a work of fiction as a platform to *try out* some of the various philosophy he has read. I would very much hope to distinguish myself from this type of author. Rather, I would hope that what I write at most embodies the philosophy I've read, and if it must try something out it tries out the philosophy I have not yet read.

Story about a father of two young children who is placed under general anesthesia for a vasectomy operation and remains comatose for the duration of his children's youth.

"Children are so beautiful! Of course there is a God!"
    "Children are so beautiful! Of course there is no God!"

The knockdown texturing on the drywall corresponds to the arrangement of landmasses on a distant planet.

"*Parenthesis or Em Dash?*: The Politics of Punctuation."

No one has enjoyed life as much as I have; therefore no one can be as saddened by the fact of death.

A critical-theoretical essay, strainedly objective, which disintegrates/evolves into strained subjectivity.

The best thing for a reader to do is read a book.

Carmen: "Ev, will you please pick up that dead bug?"
    Jackson: "Don't say that word, Mama. Dead a bad word."

Something called "Always Already."

If Carmen and I ever split up, her trump card at the divorce proceedings could be my psychotic behavior with the bedside lamp.

I suppose the ultimate goal is being okay with not knowing what being okay means.

Story in which every character including even minor and non-characters—random people in the street, grocery store clerks, garbage men—have a short story collection published or awaiting publication.

Someone should offer an M.B.A. in creative writing.

How strange that this one, instead of a different one, happens to be our moment in the world.

Short story entitled "The Obscurantist."

"I say potato, you say some word nobody understands."

We continue to insist on the possibility of an afterlife because we cannot help but insist on the value of beauty.

Extremely worried about what Jackson and Sofia will think when they read F.O.N.

The only solution might be to prevent their learning to read.

We must *unsuture* philosophy from the poem, indeed—and then *resuture* it to the book.

Novella in the form of a ledger: Pre-menopausal protagonist records sexual exploits—intercourse with at least one person, sometimes fifteen or twenty, each day—throughout a single year, 1998, using idiosyncratic abbreviations to denote information pertaining to each exploit (e.g., WOT, Miss., Rev. Cowgirl, Oral). Title: *1998*.

We will each die in the present, not the future.

I am a fully grown man who still calls them jammies.

Is my family life *opposed* to my writing life? I should finally suck it up and say, *This is my life*. Just as I am coming to know *my family through my writing*, so too *my writing through my family*; I must remember I am writing *through* my family, familying *through* my writing.

This is my life.

Something called "Scenes from the Next."

Bored to death of death.

Painting, acrylic on canvas, 15'H x 60'W: Blank canvas, save small patch (approx. 6"x6"; 8' from bottom of canvas and 24' right of center) in which richly detailed society scene appears in penciled outline.

Short story on fire, i.e., afire.

Philosophy might forever approach the limit of total divestment, the null set.

Two-act play in which characters are fragmented into many versions of themselves in the second act.

"Counterplagiarism in the Books of Married Writers."

What would actually happen here on Earth if the sun exploded? Are we prepared for that? Does the administration have an exit strategy from the solar system?

Protagonist who asks that for his eighteenth birthday his parents buy him a vasectomy.

Being is carried on the shoulders of the void.

Story about a character who never learns that the person in the mirror is himself but goes through life believing it is someone following him—which, by story's end, of course turns out to be true.

"I've never had a drug problem, but I've had plenty of drug solutions."

Which entry is really me? Always the next one.

Perhaps I should include my contact information at the end of the book in case a psychotherapist feels she can help.

Bumper sticker: "Being Happens."

"I have great difficulty reading a novel written by someone without children."

The condition of madness and the condition of parenthood have more than one thing in common.

Bumper sticker: "Poetslayer."

Life is what death does when it's bored.

Bumper sticker: "Support Our Troops. They Only Wanted Money For College."

Short story entitled "The Climatologist."

Perhaps the book should keep on until the new year and then abruptly stop.

Story about a young artist who spends much time *enjoying life anonymously* in anticipation of a near future when his literary fame will preclude such anonymity.

"My life is my little eternity."

Jackson calls the moon "my moon."

Carmen: "I dreamt last night the world was ending and I didn't have a thing to wear."

Film in which eighteen-year-old sits down on a chair in front of the camera and remains sitting until his death, sixty years later. Time-lapse photography, etc. Title of film: *Auteur*.

Nihilism is the best place to begin and the worst place to end.

Short story in which everyone in the world is an astronomer.

Not a philosophical *work*, a philosophical *book*.

After fifty years of the abdominal sinking sensation consequent to his apprehension of the fact of death, character learns from doctor that the lining of his stomach has been destroyed.

As a writer I have *evolved of necessity* since becoming a parent, having tended toward a form conducive to parenting, the fragment.

An act of parenting is an act of forgetting.

Am I going to miss F.O.N? But it's not as if I'm going to stop writing things down in notebooks. I'm simply going to have to shut up about *some book*. Or not.

Carmen on Mahler's *Fifth*: "This must be the music Hitler committed suicide to."

On Ligeti's *Symphony for 100 Metronomes*: "What is this called, *Popcorn*?"

Child playing in the house one moment, vanished the next.

Story: nervous post-grad at MLA hotel-room interview which soon (d)evolves into MLA hotel-room orgy.

Carmen is my hot Latina milf.

Father of two who commits a heinous crime in order to gain, via long prison sentence, some much needed peace and quiet.

To be led by beauty, not truth.

The word *evanescent*.

Story about husband and father of two who sells his ass on the street to make ends meet.

This year I'm changing my new year's resolution from dunking a basketball to finishing the book.

"Evan, are you really going to sit here all day and watch football? You know it isn't all about you all the time."
    "I know. That's why I'm not calling hookers over."

Epic poem in which hero floats between two stars—one in front, one behind.

"Hey Beaniebutt, whatup?"
    "Whatup, Dad."

Silver Christmas tree with black ornaments and a Raiders helmet on top.

From Old Notebooks: A Book of Ideas.

The author gratefully acknowledges
the support and guidance of Geoffrey Gatza.

Made in the USA
Charleston, SC
11 April 2010